THE BOOK OF
COPPER AND BRASS

Tinker, etched by J. T. Smith in 1815. Watched by a young woman he mends a frying-pan, while on the ground are seen some of his tools, a trivet, a candle-box (right foreground), a lantern, a kettle and other objects.

THE BOOK OF

COPPER
AND BRASS

Geoffrey Wills

COUNTRY LIFE BOOKS

First published in 1968
for Country Life Books
by the Hamlyn Publishing Group Limited
Hamlyn House, Feltham, Middlesex

Printed in Great Britain by
Billing & Sons Limited
Guildford and London

Contents

List of Plates

Author's Note

I have confined my attention in this book to everyday objects made from copper and its alloys. On the whole, scientific instruments, in the development of which brass played a most important part, are excluded as they are dealt with more suitably in specialised works.

My thanks are due to Mr D. B. Barton for reading and checking the introductory section, although I take the blame myself for any remaining errors, and to owners who have kindly allowed their possessions to be photographed and reproduced.

G. W.

Acknowledgements

Figs 41 and 75 are reproduced by gracious permission of Her Majesty the Queen.

The author also wishes to express his gratitude to the following for their generous help with the illustrations:

Birmingham Museum and Art Gallery: Fig. 24

H. Blairman and Sons, Ltd: Fig. 65

Brighton Art Gallery and Museum: Figs 40, 74, 98, 110

British Museum: Figs 4, 54

Robert Chapman: Figs 3, 5, 11, 12, 13, 14, 18, 28, 31, 34, 38, 44, 46, 49, 53, 58, 60, 61, 93, 96, 97, 105, 108, 111, 118

Christie's: Fig. 37

Devon Commercial Photos Ltd: Fig. 102

Frank J. Dobinson: Fig. 94

S. Ghey: Fig. 70

Michael Holford: Figs 1, 68c

Mansell Collection: Fig. 67

Metropolitan Museum of Art, New York; Rogers Fund, 1928: Fig. 25

Metropolitan Museum of Art, New York; the Sylmaris Collection, gift of George Coe Cranes, 1930: Fig. 10

Earl of Mount Edgcumbe, Cotehele House, Cornwall: Figs 28, 29, 31, 34, 35, 43, 56, 83, 97, 111

Museum of English Rural Life, University of Reading: Figs 68a, 68b, 88

The National Trust, Saltram, Devon: Fig. 36

Robert F. Perry: Figs 32, 33, 69, 109

Plymouth Museum and Art Gallery (Buckland Abbey): Fig. 102

E. Potter: Figs 11, 12, 13, 14, 20, 91, 93, 96, 100

Royal Pavilion, Brighton: Figs 94, 95

Royal Institution of Cornwall, Truro: Figs 105, 108

Science Museum, London, Crown Copyright: Figs 104, 106

Science Museum, London, by courtesy of the University Museum of Archaeology and Ethnology, Cambridge: Fig. 107

Dr. C. Noy Scott: Fig. 46

Victoria and Albert Museum, London: Figs 9, 15, 16, 19, 21, 22, 26, 27, 30, 39, 42, 50, 55, 57, 59, 62, 63, 66, 71, 78, 79, 81, 82, 89, 92, 99, 101, 103, 114, 115

Introduction

MINING

The mining of copper in England did not take place on any scale until about 1566, when a number of German miners were brought to the country and began work at Keswick, Cumberland. Their arrival was the result of negotiations conducted by Sir William Cecil, Queen Elizabeth I's Secretary of State, with a German merchant, Daniel Hochstetter, whose mining interests in the Tyrol were among the most important in Europe. The Anglo-German partnership traded in England as the Company of Mines Royal, which was incorporated in 1568 (Fig. 1).

In due course, the Society ventured to mine and smelt copper in Cornwall and to set up a smelting works at Neath in South Wales, but these enterprises did not prosper. Tin continued to be brought from the south-west, as it had been for many centuries, but the winning of copper would seem to have come almost to a standstill during the course of the 17th century. The Mines Royal turned their attention to lead, which was more profitable, and requirements for copper were met by imports of the metal from Sweden.

Then, in about 1700, activity recommenced through the acumen of John Coster, son of a Gloucestershire ironmaster, who has been termed 'the father of Cornish copper mining'. He devised an improved type of water-wheel for drainage purposes, and he introduced the horse-whim, an apparatus consisting of a large cage around which a rope was wound and which was rotated by circling horses (Fig. 2). In this simple manner, ore, water and miners were somehow raised and

1. The arms of the Mines Royal Company, granted by Elizabeth I, 1568.

11

lowered, as required, to and from greater heights and depths than had been practical hitherto

As the years passed, the search for copper proceeded farther and farther into the earth, the increase in depth limited only by the difficulty of keeping the lowest levels free of water. Much wa drained from mines on high ground by driving small tunnels (known as adits) that led the water away into valleys some distance away. Once the level of working went below that of the sea, thi could not be done and machinery had to be employed or mining stopped altogether.

Mechanical pumps at first were of the most primitive type, and the commonest of them was th 'rag and chain'. This comprised an iron chain to which were attached at intervals lumps of rag o leather that were pulled through wooden pipes; pipes that might total twenty feet in length and wer made from hollowed tree trunks. The lower end of the pipes rested in the water, and as the tightl fitting 'pistons' of leather or rag were pulled up inside, the water was brought to the top. Althoug the chain might run on pulleys at the extremities, it was an exhausting task to work it and nothin, other than ample brute force was required. An observer noted that 'the men work naked exceptin, for their loose trowsers, and suffer much in their health and strength from the violence of the labour' Such crude devices as this were replaced gradually by steam-engines: first that of Thomas Saver (1698), then by Thomas Newcomen's and finally, in 1769, by that of James Watt.

Cornish copper production increased rapidly from about 6,000 tons of ore in 1725 until, b 1770, it reached nearly 30,000 tons. Two years earlier, however, in March, 1768, deposits wer discovered close to the surface on Parys Mountain, Anglesey. Admittedly, the ore was not of th same high quality as the Cornish, but it lay in great quantity and was easily obtainable by open

2. A Cornish copper mine. Horse whims are seen at each side of the engine-house, and in the foreground women ar breaking ore.

ast methods instead of deep mining. At about the same date, another big deposit was found at cton, Staffordshire.

The competition from these new sources nearly bankrupted many of the Cornish ventures, but ortunately demand for the metal was strong and the price fell less violently than might have been xpected. It did mean, however, that costs had to be reduced drastically, and the most likely way of chieving this lay in lessening the amount of coal consumed in working the steam-driven pumps. ll coal used in the area had to be imported by sea, and the inefficiency of the engines added eavily to the selling price of the ore.

It was a challenge to which engineers inside and outside the county responded, and in 1776 oulton and Watt of Birmingham offered to install one of their improved engines. In the next year, ne was at work in Wheal Busy (wheal=mine) at Chacewater, near Redruth. In spite of the fact hat native prejudice caused a Cornish engineer to declare the engine was not worth twopence-alfpenny, it was, in reality, at least three times more efficient than other engines of comparable ize. In the twenty years that followed, fifty-seven of Watt's engines were erected in Cornwall, and : was estimated that the saving of expenditure on coal during the period was in the region of 800,000.

James Watt himself spent much time in Cornwall supervising the installation of his engines, ut the local people liked the Scotsman no more than he liked them. The lack of mutual sympathy vas one of the factors causing friction between makers and users of the engines: a friction that did ot lessen with time. The mine owners acquired the engines in the first instance on the understand-ng that they would pay for their basic cost, and then remit to Boulton and Watt an annual sum qual to one-third of the saving in coal compared with the amount consumed by the old Newcomen ngines to do an equal stint. There were long arguments over the method used in calculating the ums due, and when the patent expired in 1800, more than £150,000 remained outstanding.

By 1790, the ore in Anglesey was coming to an end, and from shortly after that date until the xploitation from the 1840s onwards of the vast deposits in the Americas, Australia and else-vhere, Cornwall supplied the needs of the British Isles. Then came the decline, and from an annual iverage output of 190,000 tons of ore in the years 1855–60, it had fallen to a mere 5,600 tons by 885–90. From then, the demands of manufacturers were met almost exclusively by imported netal. A few of the Cornish mines managed to keep going, mainly by converting the mineral nispickel, often found with copper ore, into arsenic for use in insecticides. But one by one they :losed and fell silent, the tall stacks standing ivy-covered as monuments to the activity of the past.

It may be added that copper can be obtained also by the process of precipitation. If pieces of ron are placed in a pond or stream of copper-bearing water, the copper will be deposited on the ron and can then be removed. It has been found, too, that when an abandoned mine has been eopened crystals of pure copper have formed on woodwork. Neither of these natural effects has)een exploited on a commercial scale of any importance, but they have sometimes supplemented nined ore and contributed additional income to an undertaking.

SMELTING

The ore brought up to the surface had to be dressed before it could be smelted and the pure copper t contained made available. An old miner described the dressing as follows:

'The first is to throw aside the *deads*, or rubbish, with which the ores are invariably inter-mixed. This process is cleverly performed by girls of seven or eight years of age, for threepence or fourpence per day. The largest fragments of ore are then *cobbed*, or broken into smaller pieces by women. Then, after being again picked, they are given to the "maidens", as the Cornish people term girls from sixteen to seventeen years of age. The maidens *buck* the ore with a *bucking-iron*, or flat hammer, by which they bruise the pieces to sizes not exceeding the top of the finger. The ores are now given to boys, who *jig* them, or shake them in sieves under water,

3. Men and women working at the surface of a mine, 'ragging, spalling, riddling and cobbing copper ore'.

by which means the ore or heavy part keeps at the bottom, whilst the *spar*, or refuse, is scraped from the top. The part which passes through the sieve is also stirred about in water, the lighter parts being thrown on the surface; and the ores thus dressed, being put into large heaps of about 100 tons each, they are then made ready for market' (Fig. 3).

Late in the 18th century, there was some use of mechanical power for dressing, but women and children were cheaper and more reliable to employ than machinery. In addition, they required no capital outlay.

14

After being dressed, the carefully sorted grades of ore were then disposed of to the smelter. The sales took place periodically, and after the quality of the material had been determined by assayers, the buyers stated the price they would pay. The price was written on a piece of paper, or *icket*, which was handed to a chairman in charge of the proceedings and the highest bidder for each mine's produce was declared the purchaser. A feature of the *ticketings*, as they were called, was that the whole business, sometimes involving the disposal of several thousands of tons of ore, might be conducted without the exchange of a single word between sellers and buyers.

On several occasions smelting was attempted in Cornwall, but the various ventures seldom prospered for very long. The weight of coal consumed was much greater than the weight of ore treated, and it was obviously cheaper and more practical to carry the mined material to where the coal lay. The nearest cheap coal was in South Wales, so the ore was sent there and the ships returned with fuel for the mine engines. Neath, Swansea and Llanelly were the centres of the smelting industry, and it has been pointed out that although Cornwall lost this profitable side of the copper trade the Welsh landscape suffered severely for it. The poisonous fumes from the chimneys did damage to everything living for miles around, and the ever-growing slag heaps completed the picture of man-made desolation.

The smelting comprised a series of roastings at high temperature to remove the impurities present, the most prevalent of these being arsenic, antimony and iron. Sometimes as many as eight

. Llangavelach smelting works, near Swansea, opened in 1745.

15

separate processes were needed before the pure copper was obtained. In order to produce a ton of the refined metal, it was estimated that between eighteen and twenty tons of coal were required, and allowing for an average of 8 per cent of copper in the ore, about $12\frac{1}{2}$ tons of raw material would have to be treated to produce it.

ALLOYS

The smelted metal is of an attractive red tint, malleable and resistant to corrosion. It was frequently alloyed with other metals in order to make it more suitable for certain purposes, and the more popular alloys include:

BRONZE – copper and tin. These two metals are often found in the ground near one another, so the mixing of them to form bronze, which has superior qualities to either of its constituents, would seem a logical happening. The ancients found the secret of making tools of bronze which were as strong and as sharp as many later ones of steel, and their use of the metal has given the name to the period of history when they were active: the Bronze Age. From classical times onwards, the alloy has been employed for making objects both for use and decoration. The comparative ease with which molten bronze could be cast led to its adoption by artists as a medium for their work, and the Renaissance masters of this branch of expression have long been acclaimed by connoisseurs.

The same metals, copper and tin, form the basis of a number of other alloys, including:

GUN-METAL, which has a self-explanatory name, but was also employed for other purposes – the making of mortars, for example, where strength and durability were equally important.

BELL-METAL, the use of which is again implied in the name.

ORMOLU, bronze finished with a gilt surface. This latter was obtained by coating the object with an amalgam of powdered gold and mercury; the application of heat then drove off the mercury in the form of a vapour. When the work had cooled, the surface was cleaned and, where required, burnished, so that highly polished portions made an effective contrast with those left matt. Gilt bronze (or gilt brass) is usually referred to in England as ormolu, although in France it is known as *bronze doré*. There, *ormolu* describes the powdered gold (*or moulu*) made ready for use with the mercury. The process of mercury-gilding went out of favour owing to the very poisonous nature of the fumes given off from the oven, and the terrible effect the fumes had on craftsmen inhaling them. It is seldom used today, as it has been replaced by electro-plating.

BRASS – copper and zinc. The latter was obtained from a mineral, *lapis calaminaris* or calamine, found particularly in the Liége area of Belgium, which gave a great impetus to brass-making in the region. In England it was mined in Somerset and Nottinghamshire from the 17th century onwards, and the roasted, crushed ore was used in the form of a powder. The resulting alloy was cast into plates or ingots, and was then further flattened to the required thickness by means of mechanically operated hammers or, laboriously, by hand-hammering. The finished product, known as Latten or Battery Metal, was made from 1568 by the important-sounding 'Governors, Assistants and Societies of the City of London of and for the Mineral and Battery Works', which operated in conjunction with the Mines Royal. Prior to that date, brass was imported from Flanders, and for a considerable time afterwards English manufacturers continued to rely on Continental supplies for their needs. Not only was the home product scarce, but it was generally looked upon as inferior in quality to the foreign.

There are a great many other useful and decorative alloys of copper and zinc besides brass, and which contain the two metals in different proportions and sometimes with additions of others. The best known include:

MUNTZ'S METAL, patented in 1832, which is resistant to the action of sea-water and discourages barnacles and other molluscs from growing on the hulls of ships that have been sheathed with it.

It was known also as PATENT METAL and YELLOW METAL.

PINCHBECK, invented early in the 18th century by a clock-maker, Christopher Pinchbeck (1670–1732), and used as a low-priced substitute for gold.

PRINCE'S METAL, invented in about 1670 by Prince Rupert of Bavaria, grandson of James I of England, and used for the same purposes as Pinchbeck, i.e. to make small items such as watch-cases, buttons and snuff-boxes.

BATH METAL was made with nine pounds of zinc to thirty-two pounds of copper, and MANNHEIM GOLD with three parts copper, one part zinc and a small quantity of tin. Both appeared more or less like the precious metal and of the latter, indeed, it was said 'the alloy bears so close a resemblance to gold as to deceive very skilful persons'.

DUTCH METAL, prepared in the form of tissue-thin sheets, was (and is) employed as an inexpensive substitute for gold-leaf. It is applied in the same manner as the latter and provides a tolerable imitation, but, like other substitutes, is not as good as the real thing.

MANUFACTURE

The several ways of making brass and copper articles were described as follows by the writer of a handbook published in 1811:

'Some of the articles manufactured by the working Brazier are beat out with the hammer, and united in their several parts by solder; others are cast; those which are cast belong to the business of the Founder, except the polishing and finishing, which require the art of the Brazier. The working Brazier has need of strength, and if he would excel in his profession, he should possess ingenuity, to finish his work with taste.

'The Founder is employed in casting a thousand different articles in brass; for which purpose he has models of the work designed: to these he fits the mould in which he casts his metal. He rarely designs anything himself, and his chief skill lies in melting the brass, and running it into the mould evenly. The Founder requires a strong constitution to undergo the heat of immense furnaces: he may earn thirty shillings per week; but it frequently happens that he spends a large portion of it in porter (a beer).

'The Coppersmith makes coppers, boilers, and all manner of large vessels for brewers, distillers and others. His work is very laborious, and the business is the most noisy of mechanical employments. The wages of the journeyman are equal to the powers of body required in the operations' (Fig. 5).

Founding or casting was done either by taking moulds from a solid model made of wood or any other suitable material, or by the 'lost wax' (cire perdue) process. In the latter, briefly, a model made of wax is enclosed in clay which is allowed to dry and harden. The clay is then heated and the wax poured out, leaving its shape inside the clay mould into which molten metal can be poured. When the metal has cooled, the clay is broken to release the object. The method has the feature that each article requires a fresh wax master model and, therefore, one metal casting differs from another. The process was, and still is, employed for the making of artistic bronzes. Hollow articles made by the same method require the construction of a roughly modelled clay core of similar shape to the finished piece. On this core, which is smaller in size than the completed work, the artist makes his model in wax. The wax and core receive outer coatings of clay, the wax is melted and the metal poured in to replace it. Finally, the outer clay is broken off, and the core removed by chipping it away.

Stamping by means of patterned dies of hardened steel had long been in use for coining when, in 1769, a patent was taken out for a similar process applied to other uses. The patentee was a London jeweller, John Pickering, and a few years later a Birmingham brassfounder, John Marston,

5. Brazing. The craftsmen are working as follows: 1. Making the upper rim of a vessel. 2. Turning a vessel to make it completely circular. 3. Man turning the wheel to provide power. 4. Tinning – on the right a man dips a pan into the molten tin. 5. An anvil on which articles are shaped. 6. Hammering the bottom of a vessel. 7. Riveting a large vessel made from sheets of brass or copper. 8. Man holding a tool against the head of a rivet while the end of the latter is punched from inside.

adapted it to the needs of his trade. Such things as the back-plates of furniture handles, keyhole-plates and small picture-frames were made in this way.

MAKERS

There is little or no information about the early makers of brass and copper articles. Their names have vanished with those of many other craftsmen, but we have a brief record of their existence and activities in a book published in 1603. John Stow wrote in his *Survey of London:*

> '. . . the street of Lothberie, Lathberie, or Loadberie (for by all these names have I read it), took the name (as it seemeth) of berie, or court of old time there kept, but by whom is grown out of memory. This street is possessed for the most part by founders, that cast candlesticks, chafing-dishes, spice mortars, and such like copper or laton works, and do afterwards turn them with the foot, and not with the wheel, to make them smooth and bright with turning and scrating (as some do term it), making a loathsome noise to the by-passers that have not been used to the like, and therefore by them disdainfully called Lothberie'.

Lothbury, in the City of London, is a turning along one side of the Bank of England from the junction of Moorgate and Princes Street. It received a mention as 'Lodebure' in about the year 1200, and since Stow's day many other forms of the name have come to light. His theory of how it became named (i.e. the noise of the founders working made it loathsome to passers-by) is an unsatisfactory one, but no certain origin has been discovered. The connection of the street with metalworking received some possible confirmation when modern building work resulted in the excavation of some copper bowls. They were found about ten feet below the present surface.

Unfortunately, although we know that such work was done in London, nothing has been dentified as actually having been made in Lothbury. We know also that there was a Worshipful Company of Founders: a body which presented a petition in 1365 referring to the manufacture of stirrups, buckles, spurs, candlesticks, lavers (ewers), and pots. All these were made by casting, and the coat of arms of the Company, granted in 1590, shows a candlestick on each side of a laverpot, the latter resembling a modern coffee-pot. There was also a Company of Braziers, whose origins go back at least to the 14th century, and whose work was carried out not by casting, but by the hammer. The Company united with that of the Armourers in 1708, and remains known today as the Worshipful Company of Armourers and Braziers.

In the early years of the 18th century, brass industries became established in the Bristol area. Not only was there ample water-power from the rivers of north Somerset, but the seaport lay conveniently near deposits of calamine (see page 16) in the Mendip Hills, coal from the Radstock district and copper from Cornwall. Among others, the Bristol Brass Wire Company, started in 1702, was able to supply Gloucestershire pin-makers with their requirements, as well as export a variety of goods to Africa and elsewhere abroad. At the same time, eager customers were provided by the rapidly growing industrial strength of the Midlands, and Birmingham in particular.

After some decades as a steel-working centre the craftsmen of Birmingham turned their attention to brass, and by 1750 their skill had established the reputation of the city for manufactures in the metal. Eventually, Birmingham eclipsed Bristol and became for many years the main supplier of brass wares to the whole of England, as well as to the remainder of the civilised world. Not only did Birmingham lie close to coalfields, but it was at the same time free from the authority of guilds and other restricting bodies.

The early system whereby a man bought his materials from the 'manufacturer' and then sold them back, in finished form, was followed widely. As late as a century ago it was still in being,

5. Advertisement from a London newspaper, *The General Evening Post*, of 1759.

and an author of 1850 noted:

> 'The system of the manufacture of hardware in Birmingham is peculiar, and presents a striking contrast to that adopted in Manchester and other large manufacturing places – the operatives are themselves the manufacturers. Hiring a workshop in which steam-power is laid on, and which is specially fitted up by the owner of the building, in which many such workshops are contained, the artizan plies his peculiar trade, manufactures his articles, carries them home to the merchant, and receives the weekly payment for them, which enables him to procure fresh materials, and proceed in the ensuing week with his regular labours. A very large proportion of hardwares is thus manufactured. But this system is not universal; and regularly-organized factories, employing a large number of workpeople, and possessing all the distinguishing features of a great producing establishment, exist, and are in active operation.'

One of the first of the true factories, in which the workers came together daily and were employed under the owner's roof, was Boulton's Soho Works, situated in a then remote spot about two miles from the centre of Birmingham. Matthew Boulton (1728–1809) enlarged a small business of his father's, built his own works in 1762, and took into partnership the Scottish inventor, James Watt. He gained an extension of Watt's original patent for an improved steam-engine, and finally they successfully marketed it. In addition, Boulton devised a steam-driven coining press, attempted the manufacture of ormolu on a scale to compete with the French, and was associated with other advances in the making of metal wares.

Although they very seldom marked their productions, we do know the names of some of the men connected with the Birmingham trade. A printed document of 1780, announcing a rise in price of their goods by $7\frac{1}{2}$ per cent 'in consequence of the late advance in the price of ingot brass', had the undermentioned signatures appended to it:

Timothy Smith	Grew & Sheriff
Samuel Parker	Smith, Cocks & Taylor
William Wheelwright	John Rotton
Thomas Underhill	Whitworth & Yates
John Barker	Price Pritchit
Townshend & Longmore	Atkins & Longmore
John Simmons	Boole & Barber
Richard Webster	William Lowe
Charles Power	Richard Beach

and Thomas Smith

Many other names can be found in directories, but they are of only limited interest unless we know what was made by their owners and how well they did their work. More satisfactory is a study of surviving catalogues, which are scarce, but can be seen in some libraries and museums. It is rarely possible to identify an example with one listed in a catalogue, but these sources do show the designs and types of articles produced by the various firms. Also, they convey an idea of what was regularly in use when the list was printed. On this point a word of caution is necessary: patterns remained current for many years, and sometimes for a century or more. This was due not only to conservatism of taste, but also because the cost of the initial models and moulds was high. It was economical, therefore, to keep them in production for the longest possible length of time. Finally, demand would fall off, and moulds were often put aside hopefully to await a further period of employment. In any case, with simple objects like doorstops and horse brasses it would be an easy matter to prepare a new mould from an existing old example. If, after a lapse of, say, a hundred years, either of these courses was followed and a new or an old mould was used, the casual buyer would detect little obvious difference between original and recent productions. Close comparsion would probably reveal a lack of quality in the finish, and a subtle variation in colour.

FINISH

Brass, copper and their allied metals can be left with a machined surface, giving a high polish relying on frequent cleaning to keep it bright. Alternatively, it may be treated in various ways to produce a comparatively non-tarnishing finish.

Copper, unless it was plated with silver (Sheffield Plate), which is outside the scope of this book, was sold in its natural state with a polished surface. This gave it its maximum attractiveness, and at the same time removed any pittings that were present and might harbour dirt. The insides of cooking vessels were given a coating of tin to avoid contaminating foodstuffs and poisoning the eater. The matter was much to the fore during the 18th century, and the news columns of the time carried reports of numerous deaths in England and other countries from this cause.

In January, 1756, the newly instituted Society for the Encouragement of Art, Manufactures and Commerce (now the Royal Society of Arts) announced that its proposal to reward anyone who could line copper vessels with pure tin had met with success. Hitherto, a quantity of lead had been added to the tin in order to act as a flux and make it flow better, but this was in itself a dangerous poison and gave no protection to the user. In the words of William Shipley, secretary of the Society:

'The unwholesomeness of copper or brass vessels for the preparation of food, and the no less unwholesome manner of tinning such vessels, with a mixture of ten ounces of lead to sixteen ounces of tin, induced this society, in regard to the public health, to propose a premium for tinning with pure tin. And as large vessels had not been tinned in this kingdom, by offering a premium for tinning, in the best workmanlike manner, the largest vessels not less than thirty gallons, with pure common tin, without lead or any other alloy whatsoever, some vessels even of a larger size, have been tinned with the said pure tin. 'Tis therefore presumed, that for the future, none who value the health of their families, will use copper vessels untinned, or permit their pots, saucepans or other kitchen vessels to be tinned with a mixture of lead, in the former unwholesome manner. For lead is soon dissolved by vinegar, or even a weaker acid, and is known to be a slow poison; whereas pure tin is a harmless metal, not so easily dissolved, will last a great deal longer, and is little more expensive. 'Tis adviseable to tin in the same manner the larger copper vessels used for meats and drinks, as well as the smaller ones.'

The maker usually finished brass with a polished surface, which gradually lost its pristine brilliance by exposure to the air. Some of the similar alloys, like Pinchbeck and Prince's Metal, were tarnish-resisting and needed little attention to keep them bright for long periods. In the 19th century, when brass began to be used very widely for ornamental objects such as reading lamps, it was usually given a finishing coat of lacquer. This took the form of a coloured varnish which not only increased the resemblance to gold, but sealed the surface from contact with the atmosphere. A typical mid-century recipe reads:

'Shellac, gamboge, dragon's blood, each 4 parts, saffron 1 part, rectified spirits 25 parts. Digest with heat and strain.'

Gamboge and saffron both gave a yellow tint and dragon's blood a red one to what was otherwise a straightforward shellac varnish. In modern times a coating of cellulose serves the same purpose.

Brass and bronze could also be given a finish with pure gold, which is itself untarnishable. This has often worn away from the friction of constant use, or from the effects of exposure to town air. Furniture mounts (handles, keyhole plates and galleries, and such French-style embellishments as feet and corner mounts) were usually made of brass. The best of them were carefully finished and gilded, but the majority were given a coat of tinted lacquer. In both instances, constant use will have worn away most or all of the original surface, and this is especially probable with handles.

Mounts to embellish objects made of porcelain, marble and other materials were made from gilt bronze (ormolu). Their manufacture was a highly skilled art of which the French were masters; not only did they excel in design, but they gave great care to the finish of the bronze prior to gilding,

7. Matthew Boulton, F.R.S. (1728–1809), after the portrait by Sir William Beechey, R.A.

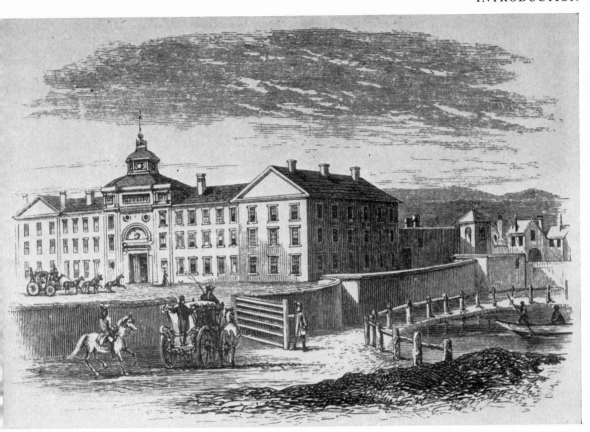

8. The Soho Works, Birmingham.

which is a most important part of the making. In a letter to his partner, Thomas Bentley, Josiah Wedgwood wrote in March, 1768:

'Mr Boulton tells me I should be surprised to know what a trade has lately been made out of vases at Paris. The artists have even come over to London, picked up all the old whimsical ugly things they could meet with, carried them to Paris, where they have mounted and ornamented them with metal, and sold them to the virtuousi of every nation, and particularly Milords D'Anglaise, for the greatest rarities, and if you remember we saw many such things at Lord Bolingbroke's, which he brought over with him from France. Of this sort I have seen two or three old China bowls, for want of better things, stuck rim to rim, which have had no bad effect, but looked whimsical and droll.'

Matthew Boulton (Fig. 7) took a keen interest in the matter, and suggested to Wedgwood that he might like to supply him with suitable vases for which mounts would be designed and made at the Soho Works (Fig. 8). The proposal seems not to have been acceptable, but Boulton certainly did mount some of Wedgwood's portrait medallions. Ten years later, he was still making ormolu, and, in accordance with business custom of the time, in May, 1778, held an auction sale in London of 'Or Molu Ornaments from the works at Soho' (Fig. 9).

In addition to chinaware, Boulton mounted marble, and some fine pairs of candelabra with bodies of Derbyshire Spar, the colourful material found only at Castleton in that county, were among his productions. Examples of them are in the Victoria and Albert Museum, London, at Saltram, Devon (the National Trust), and at Windsor Castle. It is known, also, that the firm supplied mounts for furniture which, following the long-standing French fashion, had become popular in this country.

9. Perfume-burner of gilt bronze (ormolu) on a white marble base. Designed by Robert Adam and perhaps made by Boulton and Fothergill, Birmingham. Height 21¼ inches.

AMERICA

During most of the 17th and 18th centuries the American colonists imported most of their copper and brass requirements ready-made from across the Atlantic. Such work as was done locally was on a small scale, and employed discarded articles as an important source of raw materials. A typical advertisement in the *New-York Weekly Post Boy* of 19th November, 1744, announced:

'JOHN HALDEN, Brasier from London, near the Old-Slip-Market, in New-York; Makes and sells all sorts of copper and Brass Kettles, Tea-kettles, Coffee Potts, pye pans, Warming-pans, and all other Sorts of Copper and Brass, after the best Manner; at reasonable Rates; and gives Ready Money for Old Copper, Brass, Pewter or Lead.'

The fame of Birmingham as a manufacturing centre for such things had reached across the Atlantic, and other immigrants to the New World setting up in business as braziers and coppersmiths were proud to give their place of origin as the English Midlands. In this category was Thomas Pugh, Brass and Bell-Founder, from Birmingham, at his shop in Maiden-Lane, New-York', who advertised in the *New York Gazette* on 2nd May, 1768, that he 'Makes and casts all sorts of Work in the Brass founding way'.

Following the Revolution, which commenced in 1775 and was followed by the Declaration of Independence on 4th July of the year after, efforts began to be made by the inhabitants of the new United States to make themselves self-supporting in every possible way. The products of Britain were just as repugnant as the people of that far-off country, and native substitutes were eagerly sought for the many imports of former years.

Although copper had been mined in Connecticut from about 1700, it was not until late in the century that the Waterbury brass works, in that state, got into their stride. Buttons were made successfully in quantity and variety from soon after 1800; earlier, they had been produced in New Jersey and elsewhere, but the keen competition from imports had kept output comparatively low.

10. Late 18th-century brass andirons made by Paul Revere and Son, Boston, Massachusetts. Height 24½ inches.

In Connecticut the locally produced metal was brought into use to replace wood in the manufacture of clock-movements. This was an industry that led eventually to an enormous output of cheaply priced clocks and watches, that supplied not only the home market, but much of the rest of the civilised world.

Copper and brass articles made in North America prior to 1850 are very rare indeed. Recorded survivors include warming pans by the Boston coppersmith, Charles Hunneman, and andirons and other articles by the Boston patriot, Paul Revere. The name of Richard Whittingham of New York may be added to the very short list, and quite a few pieces are stamped with initials that have not been identified. On the whole, in metal wares, as in so many other manufactures, American and United States productions closely resembled their European counterparts, and unless they are marked or accompanied by sound documentary evidence the one can seldom be distinguished from the other. It is understandable in these circumstances that the few examples proved indisputably to have been made in the country are highly prized.

Dictionary of Copper and Brass Items

ALE AND SPIRIT MEASURES Measures to hold standard quantities of liquid were made in sets (Fig. 12), usually ranging in capacity from a half-gallon to a 'drop'. Nowadays, they are to be found only rarely in complete sets, but as their use is more often decorative than functional this is not important. While 19th-century examples are not particularly uncommon, many that are bought and sold as 'antique' are of recent manufacture. Such copies are often made from a thinner gauge of metal than the old ones, and therefore are easily dented. This feature helps to give a false impression of the wear and tear that may have been acquired in daily use, and can deceive the unwary into thinking a purchase is far older than it really is. It may be added that this is not exclusive to measures, but applies to buckets, coal containers and other articles.

11. Copper ale measure. Height 9¾ inches.

12. Set of gun-metal measures (left to right); quarter-gill, half-gill, gill, and half-pint.

ALE WARMERS Mulled ale was made by mixing ale with sugar, spices, egg-yolks and othe
ingredients, and then heating it gently. Wine was also served mulled; when this was made with
Burgundy it was known as Bishop; with old Rhenish wine (Hock or some other wine of the Rhin
region) it was known as Cardinal, and when made with Hungarian Tokay it was known as Pope

Warmers made of copper were made especially for the purpose of mulling, and two varietie
are shown in Figs 13 and 14. The one in Fig. 13 is known as an 'Asses' Ear', because of it
resemblance to the distinctive feature of that animal. The boot- or shoe-shaped example in Fig. 1
is found in many parts of England, whereas the preceding kind was mostly popular in the Wes
Country. Both were used by placing them for a few minutes, when filled with the liquid, in the
glowing part of a coal or wood fire.

13. 'Asses' Ear' type
of copper ale warmer
popular in the West
of England.
Length 10$\frac{1}{4}$ inches.

14. Boot-shaped ale
warmer, made of
copper.
Length 15$\frac{1}{2}$ inches.

ANDIRONS OR FIRE-DOGS The plain bent iron rests on which lay burning logs in the open fireplace were often given some form of decoration. In the 17th century this might have been a turned capping (Fig. 15), or an ornamental boss of brass. The latter was usually pierced to form a pattern, but similar work was done on the Continent and it is difficult to determine where examples originated.

Other andirons were faced with decorative uprights of cast brass, formed with recesses which were filled with enamel. The pair illustrated (Fig. 16) bears the coat of arms as borne by both Charles II and James II, so they may be dated between about 1660 and 1689. The enamels were a type of glass mixed with chemicals to give the colour, and were applied in a powdered state. Heaped carefully in the required places when the piece of metal was in a horizontal position, the whole was heated in a kiln until the powder melted and flowed. (See also Fig. 27.)

Enamel work of this date and variety has been supposed to have been done in Surrey, but the two known brass works in the county are recorded as having made wire. Both were situated near Esher: one was started in 1649 by Jacob Momma and Daniel Diametrius, and the other, which drew its power from the nearby River Mole, was established in about 1692 by the Dockwra Copper Company. The latter is known to have specialised in producing wire for pin-making. Alternatively, it has been suggested that this cast and enamelled ware was produced in the Midlands.

Fig. 10 shows a pair of andirons, now in the Metropolitan Museum of Art, New York, made in about 1795 by the Boston, Massachusetts, craftsman, Paul Revere (1735–1818). Revere started in life by learning the art of silversmithing, but in due course took to engraving copper-plates and manufacturing wares from that metal. Inside and outside America his fame rests also on his activities as a patriot, a role in which he played a prominent part in the anti-British Boston Tea Party. Among other exploits during the War of Independence was his ride from Charlestown to Lexington on the night of 18th–19th April, 1775, to warn his fellow soldiers of the approach of British troops. The event was commemorated in verse, with ample poetic licence, by Henry Wadsworth Longfellow, whose *Paul Revere's Ride* was published in 1863.

15. Pair of late 17th-century brass andirons with turned columns, the bases modelled with the heads of men. Height 44 inches.

16. Enamelled brass andirons bearing the arms of Charles II or James II, made between 1660 and 1689.

BEDSTEADS

The brass bedstead was really constructed of iron tubing with a thin brass covering, which was polished and then coated with a lacquer or varnish to prevent it tarnishing. It was first manufactured during the 1840s and gradually replaced the wooden four-poster. At first the brass version was of the same design as the long-popular wooden one. It was hung all round with heavy curtains, and when the bed was occupied and the curtains drawn it was equivalent to a room within a room. The occupant was shielded from draught and noise, but at the same time was cut off from anything so health-promoting as a supply of fresh air.

The metal bedstead was one step towards modern ideas of hygiene; at least the material of which it was constructed would not harbour bugs, as its predecessor had done. In the course of time, further progress was made, and the all-enveloping curtains were replaced by a decorative brass head and foot. From the end of the 19th century, the Englishman slept soundly, regardless of draughts and noise, and with a more ample supply of air.

As late as 1878 an author, C. L. Eastlake, wrote: 'Many people now-a-days prefer, on sanitary grounds, to sleep, through the winter as well as the summer, in beds without hangings of any kind. It is difficult to conceive, however, that in a well-ventilated apartment, a canopy and head curtains can be at all prejudicial to health, and it is certain that they may be made to contribute not a little to the picturesqueness of a modern bed-room.' By that date, the curtains at the foot of the bed had gone, the canopy or tester was half its former size and the side-curtains came only half-way along the bed. Picturesque or not, it was not many years before the whole superstructure and all the curtains were dispensed with completely.

The hey-day of the brass bedstead was undoubtedly the year 1851, when the Great Exhibition was held in Hyde Park, London. There, R. W. Winfield of Birmingham displayed the example illustrated in Fig. 17. It was catalogued as follows: 'A four-post brass bedstead clothed in green silk, the metal work in the renaissance style, with figures, foliage, and scroll-work introduced.' The same firm showed the cot in Fig. 18, on which 'the figure of a guardian angel at the head supports the curtain'.

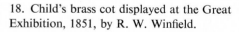

17. Brass four-post bedstead 'in the renaissance style' shown by R. W. Winfield at the Great Exhibition, 1851.

18. Child's brass cot displayed at the Great Exhibition, 1851, by R. W. Winfield.

BELLS   Bells are cast from a mixture of copper and tin that varies in proportion from two-to-one o ten-to-one. Probably most examples contain about thirteen parts of copper to four of tin, and some have small additions of other metals.

Casting is a complicated art, but a brief description may give some idea of the method employed. The principal apparatus is the crook, a fixed iron post fitted with two moving arms, one of them shaped to the inside of the bell and the other to the outside. A lump of moist clay is put round

19. Bell from Skelton-in-Cleveland church, Yorkshire, 1230–50. Height 28 inches.

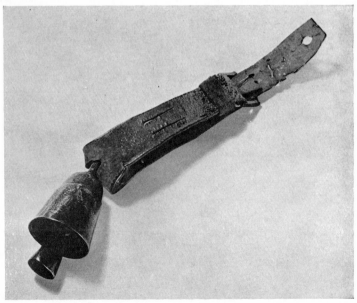

20. Cattle bell attached to a leather strap. Overall length 11 inches.

the post, and the inner arm is rotated to shape it and the clay is allowed to harden. When it is quite dry, it is greased and a layer of clay spread over it. This is shaped with the second arm so that the clay now forms a replica of the intended bell. On this is modelled in wax or clay any lettering or numerals wanted on the finished work, and then the whole is left to harden. More grease is applied and a further coating of clay is placed over the mock bell and when this has dried it is removed carefully. The clay bell is now taken away, the outer casing replaced, and molten metal poured into the cavity.

At one time, itinerant craftsmen went from place to place doing the work on the spot wherever their services were needed. Not only did they cast completely new bells, but they also melted down and recast old ones that had lost their tone, were damaged, or were otherwise unwanted. An early 17th-century book of churchwardens' accounts records an instance of the latter taking place, and notes the payment of a sum for new metal to make up the required quantity. The entry reads. 'Paid to William Lord of Chippenham for Casting of the Brasse of the Belles . . . that is to say for fourscore and seaven pounds and a half of Casting, twentie nine shillings and two pence, and for twentie five pounds of New Brass at the Rate of Nine pence a pound, Eightene Shillings and Nine pence.'

A book published in 1758, *The Compleat Appraiser*, carefully lists the cost of casting at that date, and mentions also the different prices for old and new metal:

'*New* Bells for Churches, &c. are 13*d. a Pound*, or 6*l. per Hundred Weight, viz.* 112 lb. For *New-casting* old Bells, the Bell-Founders *usually* charge 26*s. per Hundred Weight*, and then they reckon the *Old* Metal at 4*l.* 14*s.* but some Founders will *New*-cast them for 24*s. per Hundred Weight*, and then they reckon the *Old* Metal at 4*l.* 16*s.* But if the Founder is to buy your *old* Bells out and out, he will give no more than 4*l. a Hundred Weight*, which is about 8*d.* ½ *a Pound. N.B.* The above is the Price of the Bells *without* the Clappers. For new Clappers, the Founders *usually* charge 9*d. a Pound*, and allow but 2*d. a Pound* for the *old ones:* But they had rather not meddle with the *old* Clappers at all.'

Small-sized hand bells were made of similar metal and in a similar manner to church bells, and old examples are not common. Bells made from sheets of bronze, bent and riveted down the sides, were made for hanging round the necks of sheep and cattle, so their owner could trace them when they had strayed (Fig. 20).

In addition to single examples for various domestic purposes, they were made in sets tuned to cover an octave or more. The playing of them was once a popular hobby with those who rang the full-sized church bells. They were a convenient means of practising change-ringing, requiring little effort and causing less commotion in the world outside the tower. In the early 19th century a group of Lancashire hand-bell ringers played in France and Spain where, Percy Scholes wrote, 'they enjoyed great success'. The art has not died out completely, and a skilful team can provide very pleasing entertainment even in these sophisticated times.

BELL-PULLS A century or so ago, no house of any size was complete without an ingenious internal system of wires and cranks to operate small bells. Their purpose was to summon a servant wherever, and whenever, one was wanted. The bells were set in motion from the various rooms, and their noise echoed through the servants' quarters or, if all was on a lesser scale, in the kitchen. As the bells were attached to short springs they remained in motion for some time after they had been rung and, as each was marked, it was easy to locate the room where attendance was required.

The bells were operated by means of bell-pulls, which were of two principal kinds. In one, the earlier, the wire terminated high on a wall and was connected to a length of fabric or needlework which had an ornamental metal handle. The other variety was introduced later, when the builder brought the wire to within a few feet of the floor, and it was worked by jerking a handle protruding from a decorated disc. Most bell-pulls were made of gilt metal, some stamped and others cast, and occasionally they were inset with painted porcelain plaques.

BUCKETS AND CAULDRONS Bronze buckets and cauldrons dating back to about 00 B.C. have been found in ancient graves and in the beds of rivers, but their study is highly pecialised and outside the scope of this book. Suffice it to say that some are made from beaten lates of bronze riveted together, and others are cast in one piece. Most are fitted with handles.

The low three-legged cauldron of the Bronze Age changed very little in design during succeeding enturies, and the same pattern was adopted when bronze or brass was replaced by cheaper iron Fig. 21).

21. 14th-century bronze cauldron, from Ribchester, Lancashire. Height 8 inches.

2. 18th-century copper vine cistern. Length verall 28⅜ inches, vidth overall 17¼ inches, nd depth 13 inches.

The mahogany bucket hooped with bands of brass was popular during the 18th century, and i
uses ranged from holding fuel by the fireside to the carrying of plates from kitchen to dining-roor
For the latter purpose, the bucket was given a vertical slit a couple of inches in width so that th
contents could be removed without difficulty. Similarly, wine-coolers and plant-pot holders wer
made; they were lined with thin sheet-lead and raised from the ground on three or four legs.

BUTTONS

BUTTONS In the 18th century the making of metal buttons had become a sizeable industr
and it gained help from the passing of a law prohibiting the importation of foreign buttons. Th
manufacturing processes then employed were described in detail in a book, *The Complete Dictionar
of Arts and Sciences*, published in 1764, which stated:

> *The manner of making Metal Buttons.* The metal with which the moulds are intended to b
> covered is first cast into small ingots, and then flatted into thin plates or leaves, of the thicknes
> intended, at the flatting-mills; after which it is cut into small round pieces proportionable t
> the size of the mould they are intended to cover, by means of proper punches on a block of woo
> covered with a thick plate of lead. Each piece of metal thus cut out of the plate is reduced int
> the form of a button, by beating it successively in several cavities, or concave moulds, of
> spherical form, with a convex puncheon of iron, always beginning with the shallowest cavity c
> mould, and proceeding to the deeper, till the plate has acquired the intended form: and th
> better to manage so thin a plate, they form ten, twelve and sometimes twenty-four to the cavitie
> or concave moulds, at once, often nealing the metal during the operation, to make it mor
> ductile. This plate is generally called by workmen, the cap of the button.
>
> The form being thus given to the plates, or caps, they strike the intended impression on th
> convex side by means of a similar iron puncheon in a kind of mould engraven *en creux*, eithe
> by the hammer, or the press used in coining. . . . The plate thus prepared makes the cap o
> shell of the button. The lower part is formed of another plate, in the same manner, but muc
> flatter, and without any impression. To the last or under plate is soldered a small eye made c
> wire, by which the button is to be fastened.
>
> 'The two plates being thus finished, they are soldered together with soft solder, and the
> turned in a lathe.'

The writer adds that it was often the practice to use a piece of wood for the lower part of th
button, and to make the eye, through which it was stitched to clothing, from a loop of thread o
catgut. The patterned cap was filled with a cement which helped it to withstand damage 'an
preserves its bosse or design' (Fig. 23). An alternative type of button was cast in a single piece
with the eye an integral part.

23. Button-making in
progress in the mid-18th
century. Workers are
seen punching, filling
and turning the
button-tops.

A great variety of patterns was available and wholesale prices ranged from a few coppers to several pounds a gross. In 1774 Matthew Boulton's Soho Works at Birmingham was visited by Dr Samuel Johnson who recorded briefly in his *Diary*: 'We then went to Bolton's, who with great civility led us through his shops. I could not distinctly see his enginery. Twelve dozen of buttons for three shillings. Spoons struck at once' (i.e. spoons made by a single blow from a mechanical hammer). Mrs Thrale, who accompanied the doctor, noted that the buttons were '3s. the six dozen', and we may wonder who was correct.

In America, demand was doubtless met by importing buttons from England and elsewhere, but there was already an established industry there by the middle of the 18th century. A New York newspaper advertised as follows in 1750:

'Whereas I Henry Witeman having served my Apprenticeship with Casper Wister, Brass Button-Maker in Philadelphia, have now set up the same Business in New-York, where all Persons that shall please to favour me with their Custom, may depend on having the work done in the best Manner, and at reasonable Rates; at my Shop in Maiden-Lane, between the Fly-Market and the New Dutch Church.'

Wister, whose name is usually spelled Caspar Wistar, later achieved success as a glass-maker. His son, Richard Wistar, continued in this latter trade, but to an advertisement of his glassware printed in 1769 added:

'N.B. He also continues to make the Philadelphia Brass Buttons, well noted for their Strength, such as were made by his deceased Father, and are warranted for seven Years.'

Others, like 'Cornwell and Martin, from Birmingham', set up businesses across the Atlantic, and by the early 1800s the industry had become firmly established and was independent of European supplies.

The inauguration of George Washington as President of the newly-founded United States of America in 1789 was celebrated by the production of a number of decorated buttons, some with his portrait and others with patriotic inscriptions (Fig. 25). More than a score of patterns have been recorded, some of which are exceedingly rare. At the present day, button collecting is pursued keenly in the United States, and the hobby is organised and encouraged there by the National Button Society which publishes *The National Button Bulletin*.

25. American brass button made to commemorate the inauguration of George Washington as President of the United States of America on 30th April, 1789. The initials in the border are those of the 13 states which then comprised the Union.

24. Gilt-metal buttons decorated with punched and pierced designs, about 1800.

CANDLESTICKS The earliest surviving English candlestick is the 'Gloucester Candlestick' (Fig. 26), which was acquired by the Victoria and Albert Museum in 1861. It bears three inscriptions in Latin, one of which may be translated as follows: *The devotion of Abbot Peter and his gentle flock gave me to the church of St Peter at Gloucester.* Prior Peter was elected abbot of the monastery of St Peter, Gloucester, in the year 1104.

Somehow the candlestick came into the possession of the cathedral at Le Mans, in north western France, and then during the 19th century it reappeared in private possession in that town. After a few further changes of ownership it was bought for the Victoria and Albert Museum, where it is regarded as a most important example of English medieval art. Doubtless it originally

26. The Gloucester Candlestick, made in the 12th century. Height 19⅞ inches.

ormed one of a pair of altar candlesticks, but the other disappeared long ago, and it is indeed remarkable that this one remains in good condition after so many hundreds of years.

The Gloucester Candlestick is unique, and objects of such artistic merit and rarity are extremely unlikely to be met with under ordinary circumstances. The story of candlesticks of more everyday occurrence may be said to begin in the 17th century, of which good examples are certainly not common, but are still not so rare as to be unobtainable. Like the Gloucester example, some of the earlier specimens were of the pricket type, with a spike at the top to hold the candle, but by about 1650 the familiar nozzle was in general use.

A distinctive feature of the late 17th-century candlestick is the wide, spreading base, the drip-catcher about half-way up the stem, and the nozzle with or without a further rim to catch drips of molten wax (Figs 28 and 29). This pattern persisted, with slight variations, until about 1700, when

28. 17th-century brass candlestick. Height 11 inches, diameter of base 8 inches.

27. Enamelled brass candlestick, *c.* 1670. Height 10 inches.

29. The candlestick in Fig. 28 taken apart to show the method of construction.

30. Brass candlestick with a lobed base and baluster stem. Height about 10 inches.

31. Candlestick fitted with a simple device for ejecting the candle-stump. Height 6¼ inches.

a number of changes began to take place. The base grew smaller in diameter, the stem was made longer and the central drip-catcher disappeared. At the top was either a fixed rim as before or, more commonly as the years went on, a removable grease-pan.

In the earlier patterns of the 18th century the base was sometimes of a square shape with cut corners, or was designed in a series of rounded lobes. The stem was often of a baluster pattern, with one or more bulges along its length, and the pan was shaped to match the base (Fig. 30).

A refinement was a hole cut in the nozzle for the insertion of a stick to remove a candle-end. This feature is supposed by many people to denote Flemish origin for a candlestick, but an idea of this sort would certainly have been copied quickly wherever it may have originated. Later, a vertical slot was cut half-way up the stem, and from this protruded a small knob that worked a plunger inside. The plunger formed the base of the nozzle and when actuated would eject a stub resting on it (Fig. 31). A third method for achieving the same purpose was a steel rod that ran the whole length of the hollow stem, and which had a flat disc at the base. When the disc was pressed a similar

32. Pair of early 19th-century candlesticks with steel rod candle ejectors. Height 7 inches. (See Fig. 33.)

33. Brass candlestick in Fig. 32, showing steel rod ejector.

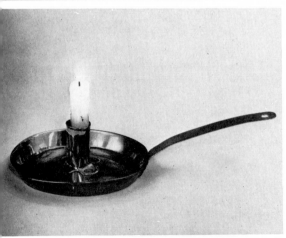

34. Brass hand-candlestick, early 19th century. Overall length 11¾ inches, including handle.

35. Adam-pattern candlestick, with fluted stem and beaded base. Height 10 inches.

button at the top was raised, and out came the remains of the candle (Figs 32 and 33).

The candlesticks described above were for use on tables, and were seldom moved about once they had been lit. For portable use, such as lighting the way upstairs to bed, use was made of a short-stemmed candle-holder set in a wide pan with a handle (Fig. 34). Often the handle had a hole provided in it for holding a cone-shaped extinguisher. An alternative pattern was provided with a tubular glass shield to protect the flame. Most of the glasses have been broken and the holders discarded, so this type of hand-candlestick is now comparatively rare.

The brass candlestick was always the poor relation of that made of silver, and the latter clearly showed successive changes in taste as the years passed. During the first decades of the 18th century the brass versions changed only slightly, and little attempt was made to mould them into fashionable forms. The rococo popularised by Chippendale had little visible effect on them and it was not until about 1760–70, when the neo-Classical became the mode, that more readily recognisable features were incorporated in their design. Vertical fluting was used sometimes to relieve the austerity of a plain column; more typically, rows of beading appeared round base and stem, and the whole article became slightly taller and slimmer (Fig. 35). At this time, also, quite a number were made from gun-metal in place of the more commonplace brass.

The candelabrum, a multiple candlestick for two or more lights, does not seem to have been made in large numbers at any period. A few outstanding examples, however, have survived from about 1770, when they were manufactured at the Soho Works, Birmingham, by Matthew Boulton.

36. Candelabrum, the body of Derbyshire Spar mounted in gilt bronze. By Matthew Boulton, c. 1770. Height 22½ inches.

37. Three-light candelabrum of gilt bronze and white marble, probably made by Matthew Boulton, c. 1770. Height 15½ inches.

38. Brass taper-stick, *c.* 1730. Height 4¾ inches.

39. Brass wall sconce, dated 1706. Height 9⅓ inches.

40. Early 19th-century perforated brass candle-holder fitted with an extinguisher. Height overall 10½ inches, diameter 4 inches.

He followed the French custom of using a piece of fine marble or rare stone for the body of the article, and mounted it elaborately in gilt bronze. Such pieces were usually supplied in pairs or sets of four, and stood on tables or on tall stands designed especially for the purpose (Figs 36 and 37).

During the 19th century, candlesticks grew noticeably fatter in the stem than they had been in preceding periods, and the general appearance became much heavier. Many of them had the grease-pan moulded in one piece with the nozzle. Far greater numbers survive from this period than from Georgian times, but as in furniture and much else they lack the gracefulness that is so characteristic of the earlier days.

Small-sized candlesticks, known as taper-sticks, were made during the 18th century. They were used on the writing-desk for melting sealing-wax, for sealing letters in the days before ready-gummed envelopes. Genuine examples are rare today. The one illustrated (Fig. 38) dates from the early 18th century and is very similar in pattern to silver specimens of 1720–30.

Wall candle-holders, or sconces, were made from the late 17th century, but very few examples have survived. Doubtless, as metal ones grew less popular and were replaced by sconces of carved wood or cut glass, they were discarded and melted down for making into more fashionable articles. In Fig. 39 is shown a brass sconce which is inscribed on the back *Edward Gore* and dated 1706. Whether the name is that of the owner or of the maker is uncertain.

CHANDELIERS   These sometimes feature in 18th century writings as 'branches', the likeness of their arms to the limbs of a tree having understandably prompted the usage. Brass was most suitable for their manufacture as it was not only strong, which was a valuable feature when lightness of construction was important, but the polished surface warmly reflected the light of burning candles. Most of our knowledge of brass chandeliers is based on those that are (or were) in churches, where they were once very common. Their popularity waned in the 19th century, and many were then discarded by incumbents who replaced them with oil-lamps.

41. Late 17th-century brass chandelier, the globular stem surmounted by a crown and the candle-arms arranged in three tiers. At Hampton Court Palace.

42. Early 18th-century brass chandelier from St Mary's Church, Newmarket, Suffolk.

43. Brass chandelier, *c.* 1760.

Later 17th-century examples are similar in pattern to those known to have been made at the time in Holland, and that country was probably the source of the earliest remaining inscribed examples in English churches. They are at Sherborne Abbey, Dorset, and at Catworth, Huntingdonshire, dated 1657 and 1666 respectively. The basic design of the chandeliers comprises one or more rows of six, eight or ten gracefully curving arms springing from a central column composed of ball and baluster turnings (Fig. 41). At the top there is often a finial in the form of a dove with outstretched wings, the whole fitting being suspended from a ring on the back of the bird. Others have a bishop's mitre or a mitre and a crown, the latter signifying the joint authority of church and state.

The most notable change in design took place in about 1740, when the arms were made shorter and fitted to the circumference of the spheres. Until then they had been hooked into rings placed among the balusters, and their greater length invariably made them droop. Also, by that date the spheres' tended to have become flattened instead of being completely round. After 1750 ornament in the form of acanthus leaves and gadrooning came into use, which was then to be seen on silverware and furniture.

Some chandeliers can be dated by means of inscriptions engraved on them, and many are recorded in ecclesiastical documents. Thus, an example at Cranbrook, Kent, was placed there as the result of an agreement signed in 1736 which authorised the churchwardens to 'purchase a Second Hand Brass Branch Sconce now to be Disposed of in London'. It cost them about £20, including cleaning and carriage. Others were designed and manufactured especially for the place in which they were to hang. Most are believed to have come from London, about half a dozen bear the names of London makers, and others originated at Bristol, Bridgwater and Birmingham.

While brass chandeliers would have been used in some homes during the 18th century, those made of carved and gilded wood or of cut-glass were more often to be found there. Brass and bronze were employed frequently for chandeliers in houses from about 1810, when the Regency fashion for revived ancient Roman styles was readily adaptable to lighting fittings. Usually they were made of bronze with gilt enrichments, and others were entirely of gilt or lacquered brass. By the middle years of the century, gas was a favoured illuminant, and the current furnishing styles were adapted to the burning of it. Visitors to the Great Exhibition of 1851 could see brass chandeliers in adaptations of Italian Renaissance and Elizabethan styles, each arm terminating in a decorated glass shade to enclose the hissing flame (Fig. 44).

44. Brass gas chandelier ornamented with figures of boys, birds and flowers. Shown at the Great Exhibition, 1851, by R. W. Winfield, Birmingham.

CHESTNUT-ROASTERS The brass chestnut-roaster on the end of a long handle looks like a small bed-warmer. Enclosing the raw chestnuts in a box with a pierced lid allows the heat to reach the contents and lets the steam escape. Also, if someone has forgotten to prick the skins, the ensuing explosion will cause no damage. Few, if any, of the existing examples are as old as they look, or as ancient as they are described as being, and it is doubtful if many are over a century old.

CLOCKS AND WATCHES Brass was of great importance in making the movement, the face and the case of many mechanical timekeepers. It gradually replaced iron, although the date when this took place is unknown. Certainly, bronze was in use as early as 1364, when it was employed for the framework of a clock by Giovanni Dondi, professor of medicine, logic and astronomy at Florence and Padua. The original clock he made has disappeared, but when it was completed he wrote a clear description with drawings of it, and from these particulars a reproduction was built between 1958 and 1961. It is now in America, in the Smithsonian Institution, Washington, D.C. Mostly, however, iron was employed for clock-making, and the difficulty of working the metal, its weight and the tendency it has to corrode prevented the manufacture of really accurate instruments. In parts of Europe, where there was difficulty in obtaining brass, it was used sparingly, and iron was inset with small brass bushes to accommodate the pivots of the wheels.

Details of the numerous improvements in clock and watch mechanisms that were devised over the years are outside the scope of this book, but the ornamentation of face, back and case merit a mention. Watches usually had brass movements, as comparatively little of the metal would be

45. Late 17th-century London-made watch in a case of gilt-metal. The watch-cock (see Fig. 46) is at the top of the movement.

46. Watch movement showing the pierced and engraved gilt-brass cock covering the balance-wheel. Made by Richard Style of London, *c.* 1770.

47. Engraved brass back-plate of a bracket-clock movement made in the middle of the 18th century.

48. Bracket-clock in an ebonised wood case with gilt-metal mounts, *c.* 1685. Height (with handle raised) 14½ inches.

required, and on account of their size they were sometimes cased in gold or silver with faces of the same metals or enamel. Alternatively, in the 18th century the newly devised gold-like alloy of Christopher Pinchbeck was used. A feature from the late 16th century onwards was the protector for the balance wheel (and later, also for the spring) known as a 'watch-cock' (Figs 45 and 46). It was given elaborate piercing and engraving in the style fashionable at the date it was made. In modern times many have been removed from discarded watches and made into ear-rings, necklaces and similar articles; this is a practice sometimes deplored, but one which gives a purpose to objects that would otherwise be broken up and lost for ever.

It was a common practice to engrave the back-plate of a bracket-clock mechanism, as such work would be seen through the glass of the door at the rear (Fig. 47). Usually, floral ornament of some type predominated and this was arranged in such a manner that space was left for the maker's name and other details. Long-case (grandfather) movements were not treated in this way, as the back would not normally be seen. In most instances the face itself was a rectangular or shaped brass plate to which was pinned a silvered 'chapter ring' on which the numerals were engraved and filled in with a black pigment. At the corners were four spandrels, popularly in the form of angels' heads flanked by outstretched wings.

The cases of small table clocks, current from the 16th century, were of decorated gilt metal. The late 17th-century bracket clock, with the newly devised pendulum, had a larger movement that demanded different treatment and was given a case of wood. Usually it was made of oak, veneered with ebony or some other imported rarity, or was japanned in black which either was left plain or was painted with a Chinese pattern in gold. Mounts of gilt metal were added; the top was at first given an elaborate pierced metal basket which grew less complex by about 1700 (Fig. 48), and was finally replaced by a wooden moulding of similar shape. The latter was often faced with a plaque of gilt metal, and similar pieces of pierced metal backed with coloured silk sometimes replaced glass in the sides. Lock-plate, carrying handle and feet would complete the article. Such details persisted when the fashionable timber became mahogany.

COAL-SCUTTLES The burning of coal (known as 'sea-cole' because it reached London from the North by boat) came into use for heating the home during the course of the 17th century. Containers for keeping a supply of fuel handy certainly existed at that date, but none has survived from before the reign of Queen Victoria. Doubtless they would have been kept in service until they wore out, and would then have been discarded. The fact that such articles do not feature in old inventories, whereas pokers and tongs often do, may indicate that the scuttle of coal was kept away from the fireside. Probably it was brought into the room, emptied into the grate and taken away for refilling.

19th-century designs varied in shape, but those of metal were usually made with copper bodies and handles of brass. A number were shown at the Great Exhibition in 1851, where visitors saw 'a copper coal scuttle of new and simple design' (Fig. 49), and 'a registered ornamental and self-supplying pedestal coal vase, presenting for use only sufficient coals to charge the hand scoop, when a fresh supply is given from the upper chamber'. Whether the inventor and patentee of the latter, Mr Harcourt Quincey of Hatton Garden, London, actually manufactured any of his ingenious vases is uncertain, but none would seem to have survived. It may be pointed out, also, that it is equally uncertain whether they were intended for manufacture in copper or brass, or in some other metal.

49. Copper scuttle of a pattern introduced in 1851.

CURFEWS The curfew is a metal cover used originally to enclose the embers of a fire and keep air from it. When the fire was again needed, a few puffs from a bellows would quickly revive it. The name was given to this simple article during the eighteenth century. In August, 1779, *The Gentleman's Magazine* printed a letter which began:

'The late Mr Gostling, of Canterbury, was a worthy man, and well respected for his good-nature and pleasantry; but, at the same time, he was very sanguine, and not a little opinionated, insomuch that, when he had taken a thing into his head, it was not an easy matter to drive it out. He was a great collector of antiquities; and, in a long life, he had amassed a considerable number of curious antique articles. Amongst other matters, he had gotten a piece of household furniture, of copper, which he was pleased to call a curfew; and his friends, on account of his years and good-humour did not care to contradict him.'

The writer continued at great length to disagree with Mr Gostling's theory that the article had been for extinguishing a fire at the hour when the curfew sounded – a summons instituted by William the Conqueror. He thought, instead, that the hood was for keeping ashes away from bread or cakes baking beneath it. The correspondence was continued later in the year, but no definite conclusion was reached. Although it is now accepted that they have no connection whatsoever with a curfew, the name has remained in use for them.

A few brass curfews, decorated with embossed designs, have survived from the 18th century and earlier, but it is not certain that they are of English make.

50. Brass curfew engraved with St George and the Dragon. Height 14¼ inches.

CURTAIN HOLDERS The tall windows, reaching from the floor almost to the ceiling in many old rooms, were draped with full-length curtains. When these were drawn apart, each was held about half-way down by a cord or a metal grip. They do not seem to have been used until sometime in the early 19th century, when the custom was to have a silk cord with tassels, secured by a long brass pin. By the mid-century, brass arms, gilt or lacquered, were popular, and many varieties of them were to be seen at the Great Exhibition. R. W. Winfield of Birmingham showed some which were referred to by the *Art-Journal* as 'graceful appendages to the windows of the elegant drawing-room' (Fig. 52).

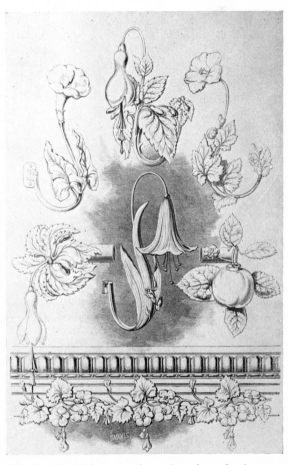

51. Late 18th-century brass curtain-holder. Syon House, Middlesex.

52. Curtain-holders, cornice-pole-ends and other curtain fittings of stamped brass with glass flower and fruit embellishments. Exhibited by R. W. Winfield in 1851.

DOOR-KNOCKERS Door-knockers began to appear on the fronts of houses at the end of the 18th century, and by the early years of the 19th century were not uncommon. Many were made of brass and their designs incorporate neo-Classical and Regency motifs: rams' heads, husks, urns, dolphins and wreaths. Some had also a rectangular flat tablet on which the name of the house-owner could be engraved. Patterns remained in use for many years and have been revived from time to time, so that many have been current, on and off, for a century and a half. Miniature knockers, for the doors of rooms, exist in many hundreds of apparently old designs, but they are of modern manufacture. Usually their bad finish (rough edges and poor detail work) gives them away at once.

DOOR-STOPS

DOOR-STOPS Most old door-stops were made of cast-iron, a cheap material that was suitable for the purpose. More expensive examples were of brass. Whereas the iron ones were made in a variety of designs that ranged from figures of Nelson to Punch and Judy, the brass ones were usually quite simple, and relied for their decorative effect on the glitter of the metal. Many were given tall handles so the user need not stoop in moving them, and all were 'loaded' in the base with a piece of iron (Fig. 53). They are referred to sometimes as DOOR-PORTERS.

53. Brass door-stop, the base weighted with iron. Height 9¼ inches.

DOUTERS AND EXTINGUISHERS For many people, douters and extinguishers are confused with snuffers. The latter were for maintaining the light of candles and oil-lamps, whereas the former were concerned solely with putting out the flame. The douter is like a pair of small scissors, but the ends each have flat round pieces to grip the wick when they are closed together. The conical extinguisher excludes air from the flame when it is placed on top of it, and does its work simply and efficiently. Chamber candlesticks, with circular trays and carrying-handles, were often made complete with an extinguisher with a square-shaped hook at one side; the hook fitted into a similarly square hole on the handle on the stem. The use of such simple devices is a reminder of the remark made about the extreme bravery of a certain man: 'Brave is he?' was the rejoinder 'then he never put out a candle with his fingers.' Conical extinguishers on long poles were used for dealing with particularly tall candles, for instance on church altars, or the lights of chandeliers.

EWERS AND JUGS A ewer was a type of jug for carrying water to the table for the purpose of washing the hands, a necessity in days when fingers were used instead of forks. A few that are probably of English origin have survived from medieval times. One of them, of bronze, now in the British Museum, has a removable cover and stands 24 inches in height (Fig. 54). On the body are cast in relief the arms of England and those of Richard II (1367–1400), and two proverbs in Gothic characters that read:

'He that will not spare when he may
Shall not spare when he would.

Deem the best in every doubt
Till the truth be tried out.'

The ewer was found at Kumasi, West Africa, by members of the British expedition sent there in 1896 to deal with King Prempeh of Ashanti. How, when, or why it reached there is quite unknown.

A ewer of somewhat similar appearance and date to the preceding one, but without a cover,

54. 14th-century bronze ewer with cover, cast with the arms of Richard II and two proverbs. Found at Kumasi, West Africa, in 1896. Height 24 inches.

is in the Victoria and Albert Museum (Fig. 55). It is also of bronze, is cast with the arms of England and an inscription reading:

'Goddes grace be to this place. Amen.
Stond utter from the fyre and lat onjust come nere'
(Stand away from the fire and let someone come near it).

Alternatively hands were sometimes washed with water poured into a basin from an aquamanile. This was designed in animal or human form; for instance as a lion with its tail curled to form a handle, the pouring-spout protruding from its mouth and a lid in the top of its head. Some of these strange-looking vessels were probably made in England, although it is known that pieces resembling them were in use on the Continent (Fig. 56).

Bronze-making would not appear to have been practised on a large scale in medieval England. A few ewers and aquamaniles, the Gloucester candlestick (Fig. 26), and some effigies of kings and queens (Henry III and Eleanor, and Edward III, in Westminster Abbey) are the most important amongst the few surviving examples of work done between the twelfth and fourteenth centuries. In the intervening hundreds of years much has probably been discarded and sent to be melted for re-use, and only chance has preserved the little evidence that remains.

In more modern times ewers and jugs, now of brass, reappeared as water carriers for supplying bedroom washbasins. For hot water a special shape was evolved with a hinged half-cover and a shaped spout. Unlike the early cast examples, they were of light weight and made from thin sheet metal which was often stamped with ridges to increase its strength.

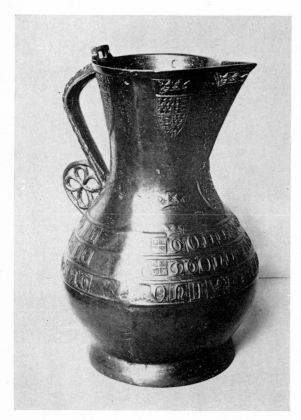

55. 14th-century bronze ewer bearing the royal arms of England and an inscription. Height 15¾ inches.

56. Bronze aquamanile modelled with a man's head and lions' feet. Height 9¾ inches.

FENDERS AND GRATES When coal began to oust wood fuel for the warming of rooms, grates in which to burn it were devised and fenders were used to prevent hot embers from falling where they might cause damage. Occasionally the iron grate was embellished with pierced and engraved brass ornament, although equally often this was of burnished steel. Frequently, however, from the end of the 18th century, fenders were made of brass. The decorated and shaped sheet of metal was reinforced by means of a base-plate of iron painted black, and in the early years of the next century the ends were fitted with posts to support fire-irons. Visitors to the Great Exhibition of 1851 could see a number of fenders of elaborate pattern, of which two made of ormolu were displayed by William Pierce of Jermyn Street, London. One was described as being of Louis XIV design 'formed of vine leaves, tendrils, and clusters of grapes, the supports for the fire-irons being branches of the vine with bunches of grapes suspended'; and the other comprised 'dogs, stags and foliage' (Fig. 58).

57. Pierced and engraved brass fender made in the early 18th century. Width 54 inches.

58. Gilt-brass fender modelled with 'dogs, stags and foliage', exhibited in 1851.

FIRE-IRONS The suite of poker, shovel and tongs, with which the fire was tended, was usually made of steel, a metal of sufficient strength to withstand the hard treatment it was likely to receive. Occasionally, examples were ornamented with brass or gilt-brass handles, and from late in the 18th century they were sometimes designed to match the grate by embodying the same motifs in their decoration. Fire-irons entirely of brass, and of much smaller size than earlier examples, were made in the Edwardian period.

FOOTMEN AND TRIVETS The footman is an alternative name for the better-known trivet; a stand for a kettle or pan placed before the fire. In one type, each has three or four legs, a handle and, sometimes, a pair of hooks so that it might be held on a fire-bar close to the heat. Alternatively, a late 18th-century version has four tall legs, often of cabriole pattern with pad feet, and an ornamental frieze. However many legs the article was given it was imperative for it to stand firmly and give its burden a steady support. Reliability in this direction was an understood thing, and achieved literary immortality from the pen of Charles Dickens. Arriving at Bury St Edmunds, Mr Pickwick remarked: 'We alight here, Sam. But some caution is necessary. Order a private room, and do not mention my name. You understand.' 'Right as a trivet, sir,' replied the trustworthy Sam Weller (*The Pickwick Papers*, chapter XVI).

Many old trivets have pierced brass tops supported on bases of wrought iron, and others are wholly of brass. Occasionally they were decorated with engraving, but this has tended to become worn away with constant use. The example in Fig. 59, dated 1668, is exceptionally well preserved and its ingenious (and amusing) patterning may have caused it to have been treated with more care than usual. At the top is the figure of Atlas supporting the world and flanked by fishes. In the lower part some of the flowing curves have been engraved with eyes and mouths and the whole complicated design rests on three little 'houses'.

59. Pierced and engraved brass trivet dated 1668. Length 23 inches.

FRAMES The vogue for portraits cut or drawn in silhouette grew widespread in England during the second half of the 18th century. At about the same time there was a demand for portraits and medallions in other mediums such as wax, glass-paste, and basaltes and jasperware. Silhouettes were cut mostly from black paper, or painted on paper or plaster; pink-tinted or natural wax was used for modelling or it was coloured realistically; glass-paste was devised and exploited by James Tassie and his nephew William. Basaltes and jasperware were types of pottery developed by Josiah Wedgwood; the first in black and the second in contrasting white and pale blue or other colours. All these small-sized representations required framing to protect and enhance them unless they were to be kept in the drawers of a cabinet.

Hand-painted miniatures on ivory were often cased in pure gold, with or without the embellishment of precious stones, and the less costly works could be framed in moulded japanned fruitwood, or, at a later date, in papier-mâché. Alternatively, gilt or lacquered brass was found to provide a very suitable and inexpensive mounting in which to set off such small portraits and medallions. Gilt brass (ormolu) was manufactured for the purpose by Matthew Boulton, and there is little doubt that pieces made by his friend Wedgwood were treated by him in this manner. Doubtless there were other makers of similar articles at the time and later, but their names have not been recorded and English frames of ormolu are invariably attributed to Boulton. The frames were cast and show no attempts to economise on the amount of metal used, while in design they reflect the neo-Classical favoured by Robert Adam and his followers from about 1765 onwards.

Small round and oval frames were made also from thin sheet brass, stamped with mouldings and gadroons or similar ornaments and strengthened with a shaped backing of pine wood. The polished metal was given a finishing coat of lacquer tinted to give it a gold-like appearance (Fig. 60). Plain rectangular frames of papier-mâché had an inner slip mount stamped from sheet brass to retain the convex glass and improve the appearance of the whole. In addition, each had a suspension ring fitted to a small stamped ornament which was often in the form of an acorn between oak leaves, or showed the rose and thistle of England and Scotland (Fig. 61).

60. Stamped brass frame containing a coloured wax portrait of the actor David Garrick. Height 4¾ inches.

61. Japanned papier-mâché frame, with a gilt-brass oval mount and a stamped ring-plate. Height (without ring) 6 inches.

HANDLES AND OTHER FURNITURE MOUNTS Brass handles and other fittings for furniture began to be used from the end of the 17th century, and their pleasing appearance assured them a steady rise in popularity. Among the earliest were the shaped corner-pieces, lock-plates and hinges on lacquer cabinets imported from the Far East. In the same manner as the cabinets themselves were copied, so were the mounts, and in both instances the English versions lacked the quality of finish found in the Oriental originals (Fig. 62).

The earliest type of handle employed on drawers and cupboard-doors was the small acorn or tear-drop type with a circular or shaped circular back-plate, through the stem of the knob and bent outwards inside the woodwork. Escutcheons (keyhole plates) appeared early in the 18th century, when the handles themselves took the form of swinging loops with a more or less oval back-plate which was decorated with piercing. Once it had been introduced, the loop handle remained a favourite for the rest of the century. Thomas Chippendale's *Director* has engravings of designs for them adapted to the fashionable rococo style, and with the coming of neo-Classical simplicity here was a use of honeysuckle, pateras and other motifs (Fig. 64).

Hitherto, manufacture had been by means of casting, which involved hand labour for finishing the surface so that it could be lacquered or gilded. The introduction of stamping reduced hand workmanship to a minimum, and at the same time resulted in a saving of metal. The back-plates of handles could be punched from thin sheets of brass, although the loop itself still had to be a solid casting. Later, in about 1790, a small-sized handle with a circular back-plate and a round ring fitted to a threaded post came into fashion. Later still came the stamped lion's head, holding in its mouth a loose ring, a handle that was made in several sizes.

By 1740 many cabinet-makers had discarded the key-plate and used instead a shaped brass piece which was inserted in the orifice to give a neat and strong finish. It has been remarked that

62. Lacquered cabinet with brass mounts and Oriental scenes on a black ground; pinewood stand carved and silvered, *c.* 1660-85. Width 54 inches.

63. Brass furniture handles ranging in style from 1660 to 1830.

64. Designs for rococo handles, from Thomas Chippendale's *The Gentleman and Cabinet-Maker's Director*, third edition, published in 1762.

old escutcheons of this type are invariably rounded at the lower (narrow) end, whereas modern ones are quite flat.

Brass hinges formed a part of the fittings of the lacquer cabinets mentioned above, and their elaborately shaped and engraved plates were affixed to the doors. Equally noticeable were the late 17th/early 18th-century hinges of shaped outline which were used on many cupboards. They were either of plain 'H' shape, or curved to form the 'cock's head' silhouette that has given this variety the name by which it is known. More often, however, the hinge remained discreetly hidden between door and upright where it did its work almost unseen.

Some exceptional hinges are on a mahogany cabinet in the Victoria and Albert Museum, London. They are visible when the doors of the cabinet are open, and are seen to be engraved with the emblem of the Golden Fleece (a ram suspended below two serpents), assumed to be the sign on the premises of the maker of the piece. The cabinet itself is exceptional, as it is inlaid lavishly with engraved brass and has heavy brass mounts as an additional embellishment. On account of its clear resemblance to two signed bookcases in Devonshire, this cabinet and some other similar pieces have been attributed to the London workshop of John Channon of St Martin's Lane. He was at work there from about 1740, and it is thought his premises may have been known by the sign of the Fleece.

65. Mahogany secretaire cabinet inlaid with brass and mounted in gilt bronze. Probably made by the London cabinet-maker John Channon, who worked in St Martin's Lane from 1737 until *c.* 1760.

The use of modelled metal mountings for the corners and feet of pieces of furniture had long been the custom in France, and with the adoption and adaptation of the Louis XV style by Chippendale and others they were rendered in carved wood. Later, however, in about 1765, not only the curved form of the furniture was copied, but also the veneered and inlaid surfaces. In this case, the metal mountings were also imitated. It has been suggested that they were ordered especially from Paris, although made to English designs, but it is probable that many of them, if not all, were made in this country.

In the early 19th century it became fashionable to terminate the feet of some pieces of furniture, notably sofa-tables and dining-tables, with brass caps. They were sometimes plain and sometimes modelled as lions' feet, but both types incorporated castors, also of brass, for easy movement of the article. Castors of small size, made for pieces such as cheese-stands that were used on a polished surface, were made of leather held in brass fittings.

66. Writing desk of unstained and unpolished oak with shaped copper hinges, designed by C. F. A. Voysey and made in 1896.

HORSE BRASSES Horse brasses may have existed in those distant days recorded in the Bible when there were 'ornaments on camels' necks'. Identification of a particular steed was important, and a favourite dependable mount would understandably have been given some positive identification mark. In addition, it would have been natural to decorate the animal on special occasions, such as jousts and parades. To hang from its neck a small plaque bearing the arms or name of the owner would have been an easy matter, and in due course some form of ornament would be added to make the whole a decorative feature. In time, only the ornament was retained, and the simple shapes adopted for it were equally simple in the ideas they embodied and the tradition they represented.

The custom of embellishing most, or all, of the leather harness with pieces of brass is of comparatively modern date, and does not go back to much before 1840.

Some two thousand different designs of horse brasses have been noted (Fig. 67), and they include countryside objects such as trees and flowers, heraldic devices, inn signs and similar emblems that may have a common ancient origin, and objects denoting the trade of the owner, like barrels and milk-churns. While the alleged deep significance of brasses is often argued at length, it is surely enough that a man should do his best to enhance the appearance and ensure the identification of his working partner. It may be true to say that the circular brasses, of which there are so many,

67. A collection of horse brasses showing many different types.

b

a

68. Horse brasses of traditional designs.

c

owe their distant origin to prehistoric worship of the sun and moon, but it may be equally correct to point out that a shining polished disc is a good reflector of light. It is an attractive object in its own right, and its shape may be no more than a coincidence.

The full regalia of pieces of brass to be worn by a cart-horse could total as much as seven pounds in weight, and the following list includes some of the individual items:

Bells: a set might comprise as many as four tiers. The Lead with five bells, the Lash with four, and the Body and Thill with three apiece. Each tier sounds its own note or chord. It has been suggested that their combined tinklings drove away evil spirits, but it is more likely that they served to give audible warning of approach in narrow lanes and kept a dozy carman awake and alert.

Crupper: several small brasses would be on this leather strap which came from the back of the saddle and looped under the tail of the animal.

Ear brasses: one behind each ear.

Face piece: one to hang over the forehead between the eyes.

Flyer, known also as a Swinger or Fly-Terret: a small-sized brass swinging loosely in a frame. One was fixed above the head and another on the saddle of the horse. Some are topped by a bell, and others have a red, white and blue brush with the bristles standing upwards.

Hames: curved and horn-shaped lengths of brass which fitted at either side of the collar.

Martingale brasses: six to ten on the martingale (a leather strap affixed to the base of the noseband and going between the forelegs to the girth. It prevents the animal throwing up its head).

Name plates: with the name of the owning tradesman were often affixed to the blinkers.

Noseband plates: small in size and indefinite in number.

Runner brasses: six in all, three at each shoulder.

69. Horse brasses mounted on a leather strap.

KETTLES The copper kettle is today not unfamiliar as an ornament of the fireside, but it is only rarely to be found in actual use. Once, it was a hard-worked and important kitchen utensil, and its principal employment was recorded in the well-known line from Charles Dickens's *Barnaby Rudge:* 'Polly put the kettle on, we'll all have tea.'

The earliest recorded silver tea-kettle dates back to 1694, and the less wealthy doubtless replenished the small-sized teapots of the time from copper rather than silver kettles. Fifty or so

70. Mid-19th-century copper kettle with a brass swinging handle. Overall height 14 inches.

71. Hand-raised brass kettle designed by Arthur Dixon, 1895–1900.

years later, a London maker advertised 'copper brown Kettles and lamps . . . which for curious work and colour exceed any that come from Holland or any other place'. They were priced at ten shillings for a three-pint kettle and lamp, and thirteen shillings for the same with a capacity of three quarts.

A book of price-lists for the use of buyers of metal and other goods, *The Compleat Appraiser* (second edition, 1758), noted that there were three sorts of kettle on the market: Brown, Hollow and Dutch. The first-named was sold complete with a stand (no doubt holding a lamp), and with a tray to place beneath it so that a polished table-top would remain unmarked. The quantity of copper in the three-pint size amounted to two pounds four ounces altogether, or exactly one pound for the kettle alone. The Hollow kettle of the same capacity was adjudged to weigh twelve ounces more, and the Dutch was double the weight at two pounds. Many of them were tinned on the inside and the cost of this was listed as follows:

'Tea-Kettles, large or small	2s. 6d.
Brown Tea-Kettles that are new Tinned will also want new Browning, and if Compleat are	4s. 0d.
But if the Kettle only, the Tinning and Browning is	3s. 0d.

viz. at 2s. 6d. Tinning and 6d. Browning. The Tea-Kettles to be cleaned of their Scurff, before they can be new Tinned; which makes These Articles come so dear.'

It seems that during the 18th century the Dutch kettle was usually equipped for use at table, whereas the other varieties presumably remained at the fireside. They varied from each other in shape as well as in weight of metal, and it is clear that the Dutch and Brown ones were not quite as tall as Hollow ones of the same capacity. The gallon size of the former measured six inches in internal depth, half an inch less than the Hollow.

Although it was made to withstand an arduous working life, the copper kettle seldom lasted for more than a few years. Very few existing examples can be dated beyond the mid-19th century, although their design frequently repeats one that had been introduced a hundred years or more before.

LAMPS AND LANTERNS Early lamps for burning oil consisted of a small open pan with a wick resting at one corner. It was a childishly simple, but messy device, and a slight improvement took place when the lamp was suspended over another similar pan to catch the inevitable drips. Oil-burning lamps of this type vied with the candle and rush-light (the latter a rush dipped in mutton fat) in giving a flickering and evil-smelling illumination. All were eclipsed with the more efficient oil-lamp devised in about 1782 by Ami Argand of Geneva (Fig. 72).

He employed in his burner a tubular wick which was held between two tubes, the inner one of which allowed air to be drawn up and feed the flame. It was found also that the addition of a shaped tall glass chimney increased the light output even more, and an Argand lamp could provide up to ten times the illumination of any source of artificial light known hitherto. Argand was trained as a chemist in France, but in that country enjoyed little personal success from his invention. In England, too, he succeeded little better.

He took out a patent in England and in 1784 proceeded to allow Matthew Boulton to make the majority of the required metal parts. However, the simplicity of the device quickly led to copies, and Argand took the imitators to court for infringement of his rights. A decision was given that the patent was invalid, and Boulton wrote that the verdict 'was hard, unjust and impolitic, as it hath (to my knowledge) discouraged a very ingenious French chemist from coming over and establishing in this country an invention of the highest importance to one of our great manufactures'.

In the end, Boulton manufactured some of the lamps. As he was by no means the only man to do so, a probable fortune from the sole rights failed to come his way. It also eluded Argand, who died in poverty in 1803.

Argand's lamp, like its primitive predecessors, used the only oils then available: those of vegetable

E   65

Clark's Patent Diamond Sideboard or Reading
Lamp.

Clark's Pearl Hanging Lamp.

72. Lamps shown at the Great Exhibition,
1851. On the right, one of Argand type in
brass.

73. Bronze Argand lamp with two burners
fed from a single oil-reservoir. The latter (at
the back) is placed at a higher level than the
wicks, and is ornamented with a satyr's mask.
At Stratfield Saye, Hampshire.

74. Brass spout lamp, 1825. The wick burned in the upper spout and any oil seeping over the lid ran back into the reservoir by the lower spout. English, after a Dutch design. Height 15 inches, diameter of base 4¾ inches.

or animal origin. The most popular was rape oil, which came from rape seed and of which colza oil is a variety from a similar source, the plant *Brassica campestris*. These oils, and others then in use, are comparatively thick, and it was found that unless the reservoir was placed above the burner and wick the latter could not obtain a sufficient supply. Capillary attraction alone was not enough, and the force of gravity had to be employed (Fig. 73).

An improvement came with the 'Carcel' lamp of 1798, which had a small clockwork-operated pump in the oil-container placed below the burner. Later, in 1836, the 'Moderator' lamp was introduced, with a piston operated by a strong spring. This forced the oil up to the burner, any surplus flowing back to the top of the piston, and the whole was regulated (or moderated) by a wire passing down from the burner to the piston.

Although these lamps gave far more light than any other known apparatus, they used much oil in order to do so. For the poorer section of the community this was a most important factor, and for their use the less expensive candle was also improved. Investigations into the composition of various fats resulted in the making of improved materials that burned for longer and did not smell so unpleasant while in use. In addition, the introduction of a plaited wick, instead of the former strands of cotton, resulted in a candle that did not have to be snuffed. Plaiting caused the wick to curl as it burned, the end of it turned into the flame and was completely consumed (see SNUFFERS).

In America, where whale oil was plentiful, the so-called 'Agitable' or 'Common' lamp proved popular. It was patented in 1787 by John Miles of Birmingham, and is of the most simple pattern: a reservoir with a removable burner in which were one or more short tubes with tightly fitting wicks. At first it was imported from England, but soon was manufactured in the newly founded United States. It was made there of brass, either with a base on which it would stand upright on its own, or with a peg to fit into a candlestick. Its elementary design made it cheap to manufacture and sell, and kept it on the market for many decades.

A lantern is an enclosed light for use where there are draughts, and it takes two forms: the hand lantern and the hanging type. The former were made sometimes from sheet brass with glass or horn windows, and a few 17th- and 18th-century examples have been preserved. Used out of doors, they usually had rough treatment and a short life.

The hanging lantern was made of both wood and metal, and there are written records of them going back to before 1600. Surviving specimens are of the 18th century and include a large brass one of octagonal shape, the top with a royal crown, which was supplied to Hampton Court Palace between 1729 and 1733 and is still there (Fig. 75). When Sir Robert Walpole was building his mansion at Houghton, Norfolk, in 1726–31, the great entrance hall was given a very large gilt copper lantern that held no fewer than eighteen candles. Sir Robert's political enemies made much fun of this by alleging it was a further example of his wild extravagance. One of their satires told how a visitor to Houghton was shown into what he thought was a glass-walled porter's lodge, and found he was inside the celebrated lantern.

Hall lanterns are among the designs published by Thomas Chippendale (Fig. 76), and there are in existence a number that were made to the designs of Robert Adam. The latter incorporate in their pattern the honeysuckle and other classical motifs that were so popular from about 1765.

75. Brass octagonal lantern with glazed sides and base, the top in the form of a crown. Supplied by Benjamin Goodison, a London cabinet maker, between 1729 and 1733 at a cost of £138. On the Queen's Great Staircase, Hampton Court Palace.

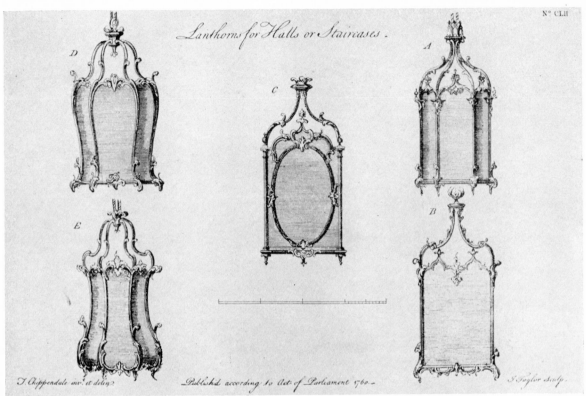

76. Designs for 'Lanthorns for Halls and Staircases' by Thomas Chippendale. Published in the third edition of his *Director*, issued in 1762, where the author stated they were 'generally made of Brass, cast from Wooden moulds'.

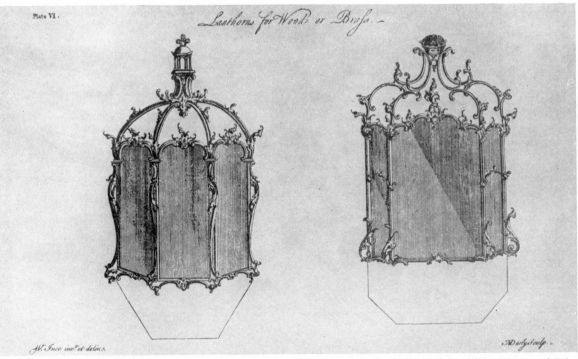

77. 'Lanthorns for Wood or Brass', from *The Universal System of Household Furniture* by William Ince and John Mayhew. The book was published in parts between 1759 and 1762.

LOCKS Brass-cased locks of the type known as box or rim locks, which were screwed to the outer surface of a door, date back to the 16th century. Examples of this date are very rare, but quite a few of a century later remain in use in the houses where they were originally installed. In most instances, the mechanism is of steel contained in a casing of the same metal which has a decorative outer cover of brass. The decoration of the latter takes the form of engraving or piercing, or a combination of both.

In the early 18th century a maker named John Wilkes signed his work with the Latin inscription 'Johannes Wilkes de Birmingham Fecit', and other locks of about the same date bear the legend 'Philip Harris Londoni Fecit', or are engraved with the name of Robert Bickford. Specimens of the work of all these makers are in the Victoria and Albert Museum, London. (Fig. 78).

Included amongst the examples in the Museum is the one by John Wilkes shown in Fig. 79. It is of a type known as a 'detector' lock and is of a particularly ingenious pattern. Pushing a catch raises the left leg of the soldier and uncovers the keyhole, while the boot on his foot points to a number on the dial. Each time the lock is used, the number changes, and it is thus possible to 'detect' how many people have operated it. The small bolt seen at the upper right is worked by moving the hat on the figure.

According to the author of a book published in 1703 the price of an average lock then ranged from five shillings to half a guinea, and he added: 'The Prizes of Locks are so various, according to their different kinds, sizes, and variety of Workmanship, that 'twere endless to mention them all; therefore I shall say no more of 'em at present, only, that there are some Locks made of Iron and Brass of 50, nay 100£ per Lock.'

78. Lock and key, with a pair of hinges to match, of pierced and engraved brass over blued steel, made by John Wilkes of Birmingham in the early 18th century. Height of hinges 10¼ inches.

Mortice locks were introduced during the middle years of the 18th century. They were set into the woodwork, and all that was visible of them was the portion showing along the narrow edge of the door when open. They had lock-plates incorporating a handle and a keyhole, one being fitted to each side of the door. Some of them, made from gilded brass, were designed by Robert Adam.

79. Brass 'detector' lock signed by John Wilkes, Birmingham, c. 1700.

80. Gilt-brass lock-plate cast with the head of George III. From Somerset House, Strand, London, of which the principal portion was built between 1776 and 1786.

MONUMENTAL BRASSES

These flat engraved brass plates were in use in churches from the 13th to the 17th century, and about ten thousand are to be found in various parishes up and down the country. Few of them are available for the collector, who can compensate himself by making rubbings of them *in situ*. This is done by placing a sheet of paper over the brass and rubbing it with black heel-ball to produce a realistic reproduction of the engraving and outline. It may be stressed here that this should never be done without previously asking permission of the incumbent.

Most or all English brasses were made from latten imported from Flanders, which was cut and engraved by native craftsmen. While many survive today, hundreds have perished at the hands of thieves who took them for the value of the metal. Soon after the Civil War, when he was at Lincoln in 1657, John Evelyn noted in his diary:

> 'The soldiers had lately knocked off most of the brasses from the gravestones, so as few inscriptions were left; they told us that these men went in with axes and hammers, and shut themselves in, till they had rent and torn off some barge-loads of metal, not sparing even the monuments of the dead, so hellish an avarice possessed them.'

Brasses have provided important facts about the costume worn at particular periods, for they are usually datable to within a few years after the decease of the person commemorated. The practice of showing men in armour has provided important data concerning that once-important male equipment. Such evidence has proved of immense value to historians, and monumental brasses have been studied carefully for many years. Only a very brief note on them is apposite here and the interested reader is advised to obtain some of the many books devoted entirely to the subject.

81. Monumental brasses to Robert Alee (died 1518) and his first wife Elizabeth; formerly in Dunstable Priory Church, Bedfordshire. Height 21 inches and 21½ inches.

MORTARS The use of a mortar for grinding wheat is mentioned in the Bible, although it is not stated whether it was made of stone or metal. By the 14th century brass examples were being used in England, where one is recorded in a will of the time of Richard II. Few examples earlier in date than the 17th century can be described with certainty as having been made in this country, and those preceding them in time were probably imported.

They were made of bell-metal (see page 16), and were the work of the men who cast bells. Both articles were made by a similar process, and some surviving mortars bear the names of craftsmen who are known to have worked at bell founding. For, like bells, mortars are found with raised ornaments, inscriptions and dates, but such decoration grew less common during the 18th century.

The mortar in Fig. 82, which is in the Victoria and Albert Museum, bears the words: WILLIAM CARTER MAD ME FOR GEORGE BEERE TB 1615. It is known that a man named Thomas Bartlett was foreman of the Whitechapel Foundry at about that date, and no doubt the mortar was cast there under his supervision (hence his initials are on it) in an interval during the making of bells.

The mortar was employed with the aid of a pestle: a rod with a rounded end (Fig. 83). Both in kitchen and pharmacy it was used for grinding herbs and seeds or for reducing anything to a fine powder or paste. During Victorian times it gradually gave place to machinery, which was not so picturesque, but was much less laborious for the user.

82. Bell-metal mortar inscribed and dated 1615. Diameter 12 inches.

83. 18th-century pestle and mortar. Diameter 4½ inches, length of pestle 6¼ inches.

PAPER-CLIPS AND PAPER-WEIGHTS Made from bronze or lacquered brass, these accessories for the desk or writing-table were produced in large numbers during the later 19th century. A popular and appropriate type took the form of a human hand (Figs 84, 85, 86), which formed the model for many other objects in china and other media. Whether that of a child or of a grown-up person, the hand had a particular fascination at the time, and the Queen herself encouraged the vogue by having plaster casts taken of her children's hands.

Other clips were in the shape of birds' heads, which were given coloured glass eyes for realism. Their beaks were spring-loaded so that they could grip papers.

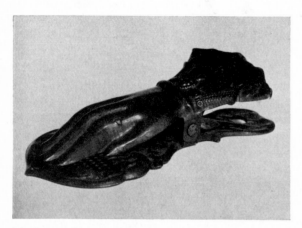

84. Stamped brass paper-clip. Length 4½ inches.

85. Lacquered brass paper-weight in the form of a lady's hand, the tassel of black silk.
Length overall 7¼ inches.

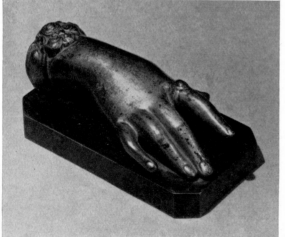

86. Gilt-brass paper-weight in the form of a lady's hand, c. 1840.

87. Gilt-brass paper-weight in the form of a horse's head with woven silk mane.
Height 3 inches.

74

POLE-HEADS From the early 18th century groups of men and women, usually sharing a common interest in their work, formed themselves into societies for mutual aid. They paid small contributions regularly, and in return were entitled to draw weekly sums during illness, and other amounts for such expenses as were occasioned by burials and other human distresses. The societies were looked upon kindly by Parish Councils as they saved many such payments being made from the poor rate, but suffered criticism from others who suspected them of being illegal trade associations in disguise.

Many of the societies, and by the year 1801 there were at least 5,000 of them in being, met conveniently in local inns, where they could transact their business as well as converse and enjoy a convivial evening. All of them shared a liking for display and held annual feast-days, at which they attended church services and paraded the district. On these occasions, all were attired in their best clothes, and in many instances the members were bedecked with silk sashes. The members and officers also bore tall coloured wooden poles topped by emblems decorated with streamers and tassels (Fig. 88).

In the West of England, and to a small degree in the Midlands, the pole-heads commonly were made of brass, the metal doubtless coming from the numerous manufactories in Bristol and elsewhere in Somerset (Fig. 89). The design of the emblem differed with each society, and some were of simple geometrical pattern while others were comparatively complex. The most decorative were those that indicated the name of the inn at which the members held their meetings. Thus brasses have survived which represent a horse (*The White Horse*), two men shaking hands (*The Salutation*), a fully rigged sailing ship (*The Ship*) to name just three.

Illustrations of more than three hundred pole-heads from Somerset and adjoining counties are in *West Country Friendly Societies*, by Margaret Fuller. Of these, the majority are in the Museum of English Rural Life, University of Reading, Berkshire, but many other museums contain examples.

88. Members of the Westbury (Somerset) Friendly Society assembled with their brass-topped poles on Whit-Monday, 23rd May, 1910.

89. West Country brass pole-heads in the Victoria and Albert Museum, London.

POWDER FLASKS

The muzzle-loading gun required charging with powder before each firing, and the required amount was poured down the muzzle prior to the insertion of the shot. Both were then rammed home and a spark from a flint, or later the detonation of a percussion-cap, set off the powder and the gun fired. The one-piece cartridge inserted at the breech, and containing both bullet, powder and detonator, did not come into use until the second half of the 19th century. Until it did, it was necessary to have something in which to carry the powder. A powder flask was used for the purpose (Fig. 91).

The 18th-century cases of duelling pistols were supplied complete with accessories which included a leather-covered metal flask. The latter often combined provision not only for the powder, but also for bullets and the paper patches in which they were wrapped so that they fitted tightly in the muzzle. Pear-shaped flasks for holding powder only were made in large numbers during the succeeding century. Some had a sewn two-piece leather body and a brass top, but most had a copper body, which was either left plain or stamped with ornament. The patterns used were numerous and, not unexpectedly, sporting subjects were the most popular.

Some of the flasks had simple lids or removable stoppers, and the powder was poured into a suitable measure. Others had spouts incorporating a device for ensuring they delivered automatically the correct quantity. Too little powder meant that the shot might fall short or fail to leave the muzzle, and too much could shatter the gun and injure the marksman.

90. Powder flasks shown by James Dixon and Sons of Sheffield at the Great Exhibition, 1851.

91. Stamped copper powder flask. Length 8¼ inches.

SKILLETS AND SAUCEPANS A skillet is a cooking-pot supported on three feet and with a long handle. It was designed for use on a cottage hearth, for the feet kept it off the ground and above the glowing ashes, and the handle enabled it to be removed when necessary without burning the hand. They were made of bell-metal and, like mortars, were a production of the bell-founders who habitually ornamented their work with names or inscriptions. The earliest skillets were bowl-shaped, but by the 17th century the sides had become straight, and this type is the one seen occasionally today. The handle was the part to receive embellishment, which was cast in the making. When it did not take the form of a name, with or without a date, it was usually a grim reminder that YE WAGES OF SIN IS DEATH (Fig. 92), or the poignant injunction PITTY THE POORE.

Saucepans of the type used today, with flat bases and upright sides, came into use during the late 18th century (Fig. 93). Copper was usually employed in making them, and they were heavily

92. Bell-metal skillet, the handle cast with the words 'Ye Wages of Sin is Death'. Length 16½ inches.

93. Copper saucepan and cover, the interior tinned. Diameter 5¼ inches.

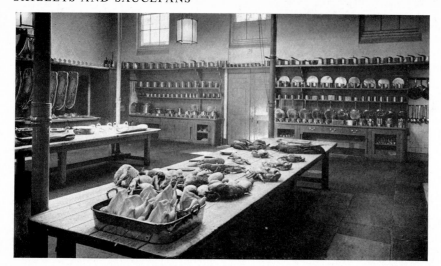

94. The Kitchen, Royal Pavilion, Brighton, Sussex.

95. Copper bain-marie for cooking separate foods in hot water. The initials and coronet on the front indicate that it was included in the Duke of Wellington's inventory. From the Kitchen, Royal Pavilion, Brighton. (See Fig. 94.)

tinned on the insides to prevent poisoning. In spite of this, there was much concern about the use of impure tin alloys which contained a proportion of lead, and therefore did nearly as much damage to health as the bare copper (see page 21).

The kitchens of great houses were equipped with large sets of saucepans, complete with pans of every kind and moulds for sponges and other delicacies. These were made of copper kept brilliantly polished, ready for use, and making a dazzling display. Visitors to the Kitchen at the Royal Pavilion, Brighton (Fig. 94), will recollect the fine *batterie-de-cuisine* shown there. It once belonged to the Duke of Wellington, the 'Iron Duke', and each piece bears his insignia (Fig. 95).

SKIMMERS   The skimmer has a slightly concave, circular bowl of brass pierced with holes. Most of them have a long iron handle with a hook or hole at the end for suspension (Fig. 96). A variety has a ring handle affixed at one side.

They were used for skimming cream from milk in the days when the latter was poured into large wide-topped pans. These allowed the cream to rise and then it could be removed for butter making or any other purpose.

96. Brass skimmer with an iron handle. Length 33½ inches.

SNUFFERS In the days when the candle had a wick that did not get consumed in the flame, it was essential to keep the wick trimmed short. Otherwise, it would bend over to the edge of the candle causing the wax to melt and drip, and at the same time emit black smoke. Trimming was done by means of a pair of snuffers: a scissors-like device which not only cut the wick to the required length, but also gripped the unwanted and offending end.

Early 18th century snuffers were made of brass, and occasionally survive complete with their original stands (Fig. 97). Later in the century brass ones were made less often, and their place was taken by plated examples. These often had ingenious cutters as well as little boxes for automatically holding the discarded wick ends.

97. Pair of brass snuffers and stand, mid-18th century. Height of stand 4¾ inches, length of snuffers 5½ inches.

SPIT-JACKS In early times, meat was roasted in front of the fire, and for the purpose was fixed to the prongs of an iron spit or contained in a metal spit-basket. To ensure even cooking it was rotated either by a fan in the chimney, which revolved because of the ascending hot air and smoke, or by a turn-spit: a term used indiscriminately for a child or a dog employed at the dreary task. By the end of the 17th century the spit-jack had been evolved. It took the form of a simple mechanism driven, like a large clock, by a falling weight. Later still, a spring-driven version was introduced, and this was much smaller in size than any other type. It was cased in brass, and because of its shape was called a 'bottle-jack' (Fig. 98).

98. 19th-century brass-cased clockwork spit or 'bottle-jack' for suspending a joint before an open fire, or in a Dutch oven.

SPOONS On 23rd September, 1567, the Court of the Pewterers' Company agreed that 'there should be no spoons made of brass or latten or any yellow metal, upon pain that if any person hereafter be found that he does make any such spoons shall forfeit and pay for every spoon ¾d. The said spoons were lately invented by John God, and he has confessed he has made but three dozen; one dozen he has sold to one in Aldgate, and another stranger has bought one other dozen. And the third dozen the good man of the Castle in Wood Street must have them. And if there be found any more of the same God's making, he shall pay for every spoon ¾d.'

With orders like the above, and others of a similar nature, it is not surprising that brass spoons of the period are rare. Survivors from the succeeding 17th century are also far from plentiful, but specimens are brought to light from time to time. Usually they are found during excavations, which recover them from where they were long ago lost or discarded. Many thousands of them must

99. 14th- and 15th-century latten spoons and a two-pronged fork.

have been thrown aside when worn or unfashionable, and when sold as scrap metal would have been melted and converted into other articles.

Old brass spoons are comparable in shape to those of pewter and silver of the same date. Their handles terminate in a variety of ornamental knobs, which include the following:

Cone: resembling a fir-cone.
Slipped in the Stalk: cut off at an angle.
Wrythen: a ball with spiral cuts.
Seal: circular with a flat top.
Apostle: a standing figure of an apostle.
Lion: a seated lion.
Acorn ⎫
Diamond-point ⎭ : self-descriptive.

Towards the end of the 17th century the bowl of the spoon became more oval in shape than it had been, and the handle frequently ended in a trifid: rounded and with two notches cut in it.

Many old spoons were finished with a coating of tin and marked in a manner similar to those of silver, but nothing is known of their makers.

WARMING PANS Our ancestors took great care that they should be warm in bed. In addition to hanging heavy curtains all round the bedstead until it resembled a room inside a room, they did what they could to take the chill off the bedding. For this purpose, they used a covered metal pan containing glowing charcoal, and which had a long handle so that it could be pushed well down between the sheets and blankets. The hinged covers of the pans were pierced to allow air to reach the charcoal, and the necessary holes were usually formed into a decorative pattern. Additional ornament took the form of engraving which sometimes incorporated an inscription and, occasionally, initials and a date.

The earlier examples which were made in the 17th century had handles of iron (Fig. 101). When these latter had brass embellishments, it has been suggested they were of Continental origin and that only plain ones were made in England. There would seem to be no proof of the truth or otherwise of this assertion. 18th-century warming pans were given handles of turned beech or other timber, usually finished with a coat of black japan. Both copper and brass were used indiscriminately for the pans and covers. While they are seldom, if ever, employed for their original function nowadays, a large number have been preserved and hang on walls for decoration.

100. 19th-century pierced and punched copper warming pan fitted with a wooden handle.

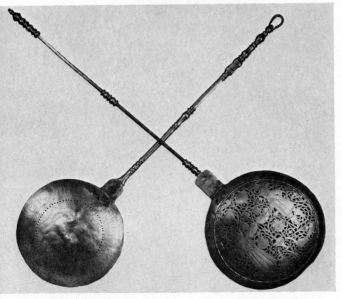

101. Two 17th-century brass warming pans with iron handles. The left-hand one inscribed 'The Earle of Essex his Arms', and the right-hand one engraved with figures, birds and flowers.
Length 43 inches and 47¾ inches.

WEIGHTS AND MEASURES

Bronze was used for many centuries for making the sets o standard weights and measures issued to cities and towns. In 1495, in the reign of Henry VII, it wa ordered that they be delivered at the royal expense 'to all members of Parliament, knights of th shire, barons of the Cinque Ports, as burgesses of borough towns, to be deposited in all cities towns corporate, and other convenient boroughs and towns having a constable, throughout thei several districts, there to be and remain for ever as standards'.

At that date it was declared officially that 'the measure of a bushel shall contain 8 gallons o wheat, and that every gallon shall contain 8lbs. of wheat of Troy weight, and every pound contai 12 ounces of Troy weight, and every ounce contain 20 sterlings [better known as pennyweights dwts.], and every sterling be of the weight of 32 corns [grains] of wheat that grow in the midst o the ear of wheat, according to the old law of this land'. The Troy weight referred to was name after Troyes, in eastern France, where the Roman standard of 24 barleycorns to an ounce had bee adopted.

In spite of the elaborate wording used above in defining the weights and capacities, the basi standard, a grain of wheat, inevitably led to discrepancies between one measure and another These were increased by wear and tear and sheer age, which distorted and otherwise damaged th articles. Slackness of administration led to the employment of different measures in differen parts of the country, and at one period there were as many as four standard bushels. All of them were legal, and they were used for beer, wine, coal and corn. They were of a capacity varying from eight to twelve gallons, according to which of the products was being dealt with.

The old standard measures invariably bear the name of the city or town in which they were used the date of issue, and the capacity (Fig. 102). They are very strongly made, and a gallon measure is no light weight to lift off the ground.

Wool, which was once the most important of the country's products, had the benefit of specially shaped bronze weights (Fig. 103). They were used in assessing it for taxation at the specified stapl

102. Standard measures dated 1826. (Left to right), half-bushel, bushel, and peck.

owns, where all the fleece of the surrounding districts had to be submitted to the royal scales. Wool was weighed by the Tod of 28 pounds, and further by the Sack, the Weigh, the Stone, and the Clove. Bronze wool weights bear the coat of arms of the reigning monarch, together with the stamp of the Founders' Company and marks impressed by the authorities in London and elsewhere. At the back of each can be seen a circular hollow made when surplus metal was removed by the maker. This was done to ensure that the weight matched the standard.

Wool weights were changed with each succeeding monarch, and it was a rule that the disused ones should be destroyed. Often this was disobeyed, and quite a few have been preserved. Their numbers have been increased by forgeries, and a collector should be on his guard against them.

103. Wool weight of 14 pounds modelled with the arms of Queen Elizabeth I. Height $7\frac{1}{2}$ inches.

104. Queen Elizabeth's standard bronze avoirdupois weights; third series, 1588. The bell-shaped weights are from 56 lb. to 1 lb. and the flat weights from 8 lb. to 2 drams.

105. Bronze weight with iron handle, dated 1705. 1¾ inches square.

106. English apothecaries' pocket scales and weights in fish skin covered case, *c.* 1750. Height of scales about 4 inches.

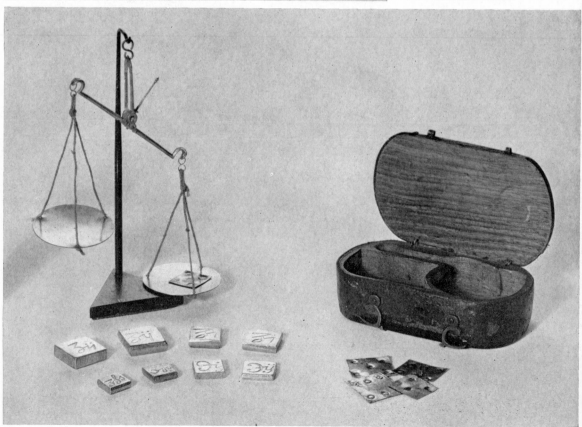

107. Nest of avoirdupois weights, 28 lb. to 2 drams, dated 1773.

108. Early 19th-century nest of weights in a shagreen case. The weights are 8 ounces, 4 ounces, 2 ounces, 1 ounce, 8 drams, 4 drams and 2 drams.
Height of box 2¼ inches.

MISCELLANEOUS   The principal articles made from brass and copper have been described in the foregoing glossary, but there remain a number of others. In most instances they are only rarely seen and in others little is known about them, so little information can be recorded. For these reasons it is convenient to group them together under the heading of Miscellaneous.

Many small-sized **Tobacco Boxes** were of foreign manufacture, which is often quite clear from the inscriptions engraved or stamped on them, but some were made in England. There is a record of Matthew Boulton having supplied a large number to the East India Company, 'which he was enabled to do by making them of Bath metal, which admitted of being struck when hot in very handsome forms; they could not have been made of brass at twice the money'. Smokers were catered for also by the provision of **Pipe Stoppers** in many designs. They were used for pressing down the tobacco in the pipe-bowl, and had a flat rounded top which made them resemble a seal. Brass was often used for making them, but as they were small, so that they could be carried in the pocket, they were easily lost and are now quite rare.

Candle Boxes, tubular and with hinged lids, were made for hanging on a wall where they could hold a supply of candles ready for use when needed. For providing a source of heat sufficient for melting sealing-wax or for any other purpose, a **Wax-Jack** (Fig. 111) was sometimes used instead of a candle. It held a coil of wax taper (in a length of a yard or so) which was unwound as required and fed up through a hole in a nozzle. Most surviving examples are of silver, but they were made also of brass, and sometimes old examples in the latter material have been preserved.

Pocket **Coin Balances** were used to test the genuineness of gold sovereigns and half-sovereigns in the days when these coins were current. They were placed in one end of the balance which could

109. Brass fitting for hanging a pot over a fire while cooking.

110. Late 18th-century brass 'strike-a-light', the forerunner of the modern match. It was fired like a pistol to ignite the cotton or linen fabric in the pan, which could then be used to light a sulphur 'match' stored in the barrel.

111. Brass wax-jack, the winding spindle missing. Dated 1702. Length 8½ inches.

112. Pocket balance, with brass pans and steel arm, in a shagreen-covered case. *c.* 1790. Length of case 5¼ inches.

113. Maker's label in the lid of the scale-case shown in Fig. 112.

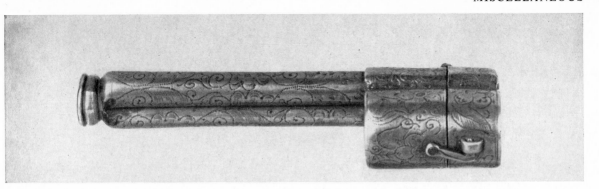

114. Two brass pen and sealing-wax cases, the upper one dated 1652 and the lower one 1656. Length about 4½ inches.

be set to test the weight of one or more values of coin and provided a quick means of combating forgeries. The balances were of small size, and some folded neatly into a leather case to protect them from damage when in the pocket (Figs 112 and 113).

Two 17th-century brass **Pen Cases** for holding pens and sealing-wax are in the Victoria and Albert Museum (Fig. 114). They are engraved with floral and other designs, including animal heads. On one is inscribed: 'Virgo me fecit Sheffeild, 1652', and on the other: 'I was in Sheffeild made & many can Witness: I was not made by any man', the date 1656 and initials I.D. They are supposed to have been the handiwork of a member of a well-known family of Sheffield cutlery makers, named Madin or Maden. It would seem that he humorously employed a Latin version of his surname (*virgo: maiden*) to inscribe on these examples of his craftsmanship.

Useful domestic articles, like the pair of sugar-casters and the milk or cream jug in Fig. 115, must have existed at one time in large numbers. Today they are very scarce, as when their owners thought them to be of unfashionable design they would have sent them away as scrap metal. All three of the pieces illustrated resemble silver examples, which can be dated from their hall-marks to the middle of the 18th century. The brass ones were made during the same period.

The heat from a well stoked fire or the light from a carefully trimmed lamp could trouble the sensitive, and to protect them from irritations there were portable **Screens.** They could be placed where they would protect the face and eyes, and would seem to have been popular in the middle years of the 19th century. The one illustrated in Fig. 116 is a particularly attractive example, with telescopic adjustment for height as well as a hinge so that it can be angled. It screws together after being taken from its leather-covered travelling case, which measures 6⅞ by 2¼ inches and has the interior lined neatly in red velvet. The pleated screen is of green silk, and the polished brasswork lacquered so that it remains untarnished to this day.

Being comparatively soft metals, brass and copper must always have attracted amateur crafts-

115. Mid-18th-century pair of brass casters and a cream jug. Height 4½ inches and 9⅛ inches.

men. However, it is not always easy to distinguish their work from that of professionals. The **Watch Holder** in Fig. 117 is possibly amateur work, as there would surely not have been a large enough demand for an article of such individual design to have been manufactured commercially. It dates from sometime in the second half of the 19th century, and must once have stood gleaming on a mantelpiece proclaiming the skill of its maker to all who sought the time of day.

Also perhaps the work of enthusiastic home-craftsmen were such brass objects as miniature tables, fenders and other **Toys** (Fig. 118). It has been argued that such things may have been made in workshops for dolls' houses, or were apprentice test-pieces, or travellers' samples, but there remains no proof of any of these theories. The idea that a metal-worker might spend some of his leisure time making playthings for his children is certainly equally acceptable. In any case, many of these little objects are very well made and much more practical than wooden ones; they stand up to a hard life, but it must be added that not all of them are as old as they seem to be.

116. Table screen with green silk pleated shade, the box to contain it covered in red leather. Height $15\frac{1}{2}$ inches, extending to 23 inches. Box $2\frac{1}{4}$ inches by $6\frac{7}{8}$ inches.

117. Late 19th-century cut-out brass watch-holder in the form of a pair of buttoned boots. Length $8\frac{1}{2}$ inches.

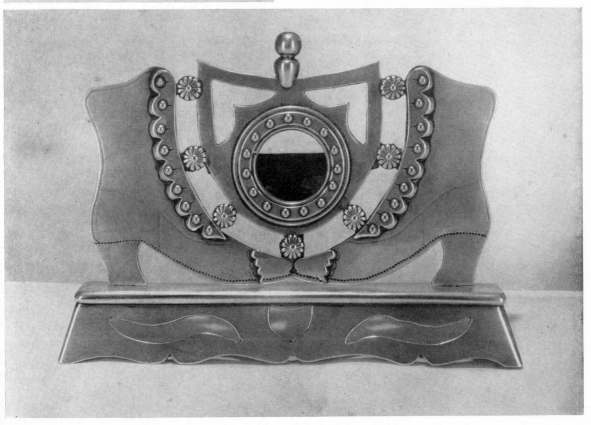

118. 19th-century stamped brass toy wax-jack. Height 1 inch.

Selected Bibliography

Barton, D. B.   *A History of Copper Mining in Cornwall and Devon*, Truro, 1961.

Clark, Victor S.   *History of Manufactures in the United States, 1607–1860*, Washington, D.C., 1916.

Dickinson, H. W.   *Matthew Boulton*, 1937.

Fuller, Margaret   *West Country Friendly Societies*, Lingfield, 1964.

Hamilton, Henry   *The English Brass and Copper Industries to 1800*, 1926.

Larkin, James   *The Practical Brass and Iron Founders' Guide*, second edition, Philadelphia, 1853.

Liefchild, J. R.   *Cornwall: Its Mines and Miners*, 1860.

Lindsay, J. Seymour   *Iron and Brass Implements of the English House*, 1927, reprinted 1965.

Macquoid, P., and Edwards, Ralph   *The Dictionary of English Furniture*, 3 vols, second edition revised by Ralph Edwards, 1954.

Mann, James   *Monumental Brasses* (King Penguin), 1957.

Oman, Charles   *The Gloucester Candlestick*, H.M.S.O., 1958.

Peck, E. Saville   *Notes upon a Cambridge Collection of Bell Metal Mortars* (Cambridge Antiquarian Society's Communications, vol. 32), 1932.

Redding, Cyrus   *An Illustrated Itinerary of the County of Cornwall*, 1842.

V. and A. Museum: *Old English Pattern Books of the Metal Trades*, 1913.

Worth, B. N.   *Historical Notes concerning the Progress of Mining Skill in Devon and Cornwall*, Falmouth, 1872.

Index

Page numbers in italics refer to illustrations.